CONTAINER GARDENS

COMPLETE GARDENER'S LIBRARY™

CONTAINER

GARDENS

Barbara Pleasant

with
Doreen Howard
and Betty Mackey

**National Home
Gardening Club**
Minneapolis, Minnesota

Container Gardens

Copyright ©1997 National Home Gardening Club

Mike Vail
Vice President, Product & Business Development

Tom Carpenter
Director of Book Development

A. Cort Sinnes
Home Gardener's Library Executive Editor

Dan Kennedy
Book Production Manager

Michele Teigen
Senior Book Development Coordinator

Justin Hancock

Julie Lindemann

Molly Rose Teuke
Content Editors

David J. Farr, ImageSmythe
Series Design, Art Direction and Production

Photo Credits

William D. Adams: 25, 19, 36, 111; Jim Block: 75; David Cavagnaro: 18, 63, 66, 67, 104, 122, 139(2); Walter Chandoha: 5, 4, 7, 24(3), 27(2), 26, 20, 23, 22(3), 12, 19, 21(2), 39, 40, 57, 58, 61, 60, 62, 65, 64, 67, 66, 69, 76, 79, 80, 84, 86, 89, 90, 93(2), 92, 95(2), 96, 97, 98, 103, 107, 106, 114, 117, 121, 133; Rosalind Creasy: 13, 12, 17, 62, 66, 68, 77, 81, 102, 108, 112, 115, 117; Thomas E. Eltzroth: 22, 42, 58, 91, 94, 112, 121, 123, 122, 128, 131, 138; Derek Fell: cover, 5, 27(2), 26, 21, 20, 23, 22, 25(3), 24, 18, 35, 34, 39, 50, 55, 57, 56, 59, 58, 61(2), 60(2), 63, 65, 64, 66, 69, 76, 78(2), 81, 80, 83(2), 85(2), 84, 91, 114, 116(2), 120(2), 129, 130, 133, 137, 136, 138(2), 139(3), 140; Saxon Holt: vi, 4, 24, 26, 23, 25, 12, 15, 17(2), 18, 21, 31, 41(2), 70-71, 71, 83, 101(2), 127, 137, 138; Michael Landis: v, 4, 6, 9, 10, 11, 24(2), 15, 16, 18, 30, 45(3), 44(3), 47(2), 48(2), 49(2), 77, 113, 112, 117, 121, 138; Maggie Oster: 4, 8, 26, 20(4), 23(2), 13, 15(2), 17, 19, 28, 61, 60, 64(2), 69, 68, 75, 81, 100, 103, 102, 105, 107, 123, 136; Jerry Pavia: 2, 6, 21(2), 12, 14, 16(3), 19(2), 54, 59(2), 67, 66, 80, 82, 106, 124, 129(2), 131, 132, 136, 138; Robert Perron: 26; Stephen R. Swinburne: 32; Mark Turner: 37, 68, 134; Hugh Palmer: 7, 24, 23(2), 12, 19, 31, 81, 120; Betty Mackey: 77.

4 5 6 7 8 9 / 05 04 03 02 01

ISBN 0–914697–97–8

National Home Gardening Club
12301 Whitewater Drive
Minnetonka, Minnesota 55343

www.gardeningclub.com

CONTENTS

CHAPTER 10

Roses, Shrubs and Trees 125

CHAPTER 11

Theme Container Gardens 135

CHAPTER 12

Pests and Diseases in Container Gardens 141

References

New Perspectives on Container Gardening

*A*lmost any plant that can be grown in the ground can be grown in containers, and some even grow better that way. Container gardening is easy, too. You can forget about heavy digging and weeding, and still fill your outdoor spaces with plants that are beautiful, fragrant or wonderful to eat.

Container gardening is a perfect fit for many people who lack the space or time for growing big borders or large vegetable beds. In container gardening, all you need is a little spot of sun on a deck or balcony, or perhaps a narrow strip of space in a small city lot. Yet container gardening also attracts gardeners who simply enjoy the ease and almost assured success of growing plants in pots. The truth be told, you can do things in container gardening that are rarely possible when plants are grown in the ground.

Container gardens are concentrated gardens, which is certainly part of their appeal. Whether the site is a courtyard or a window box, you can use plants in containers to evoke the lush feel of a much larger collection of plants. A single strawberry pot planted with succulent sedums and sempervivums becomes a desert oasis when set on a concrete patio. In similar fashion, a shady corner packed with colorful coleus and caladiums cannot help but feel like a tropical retreat.

Container gardens are adventurous undertakings, complete with thrilling risks and extraordinary rewards. Certainly you may get started in container gardening by adopting a few plants you truly love and using them to furnish your outdoor space. But then something strange often happens, and you find yourself yearning for new experiences, new worlds to conquer. From a small pot of petunias, you graduate to creating an exotic container bouquet. Before long, burying bulbs shoulder to shoulder in soft potting soil becomes an annual fall ritual, or perhaps herbs steal their way into your gardening heart. Like the gardeners who grow them, container gardens are always ready for change.

Container gardening is easy, for every aspect of your plants' lives are within your control. Proceed thoughtfully, and you are almost assured of success—without the usual quota of hard physical labor needed to grow a great garden. Countless modern gardeners have used every trick known to reduce the maintenance required by their outdoor landscapes, and then turned to container-grown plants for exciting color and low-labor gardening fun.

THREE VOICES, THREE VIEWS

The information in this book is based on the first-hand experiences of three authors, each of whom is delighted to share her passion for container gardening. I am Barbara Pleasant, the primary author, and let me confess from the outset that I have yet to find a type of gardening that I do not adore. At the same time, I know that I am a focal-point gardener at heart. I love growing little pictures with plants, combining colors and textures and forms to create smashing compositions that make me smile each time I see them. At my house, dinner is apt to run late on days when I fill or rearrange pots, or when much smaller things happen, such as the little lotus in my water garden revealing its first bloom.

Consider this fair warning that I have tried my best to make sure this book infects every reader with my own tendency toward an obsessive type of gardening where breathtaking beauty is the ultimate goal.

For growing edibles in containers, you could ask for no finer mentor than Doreen Howard, who started gardening twenty years ago in two foam ice chests, a plastic wash tub and a few

Barbara Pleasant

weathered flower pots on a second-floor apartment landing in Hollywood, California. Soon pole beans, cherry tomatoes, parsley, carrots, lettuce, marigolds and strawberries filled the landing. From that small beginning came Doreen's 20-year love affair with container gardening. She has grown hundreds of plants in containers, and won a trophy at the Texas State Fair with a two-pound heirloom tomato grown in a pot. Today, her flagstone courtyard is a celebration of tub-grown fruits, including peaches, bananas, figs and citrus.

The third voice you will hear in these pages is that of Betty Mackey, a well known writer whose half-acre Pennsylvania yard is filled with hundreds of perennials and bulbs. The plants in Betty's garden beds struggle against shade, but not those in containers on her stone terrace, which basks in the sun. "I have found that I like the way many of my favorite plants look in containers," Betty says. "In containers, I get inspired to try more aesthetic ways to use perennials and bulbs." Also a seasoned plant propagator, Betty uses a secret niche in her narrow side yard as a little potting workshop, like a miniature nursery. Many of Betty's baby plants find their way to her local garden club's annual plant sale, which funds a college scholarship.

Now that this book is complete, all three of us do have one common problem: A raging desire to plant every slip, seed and root you are about to discover within these pages. We cannot help ourselves. We must garden, as much as we must eat and sleep. And we find tremendous satisfaction by gardening in pots.

Barbara Pleasant

Chapter 1

❧

CONTAINER GARDENING PAST AND PRESENT

Growing plants in containers is an ancient art that has developed into something new and different to fit the modern age. Go back in time one hundred years, and you would find European parlors graced with geraniums coaxed into bloom all winter in sunny windowsills. Jump back three centuries, and if you were so lucky to be invited to spend time in a fine Italian villa, you might encounter carefully tended citrus trees, grown in some of the first terra-cotta pots.

We can only imagine what these container gardening pioneers would think of today's lush container bouquets packed with beautiful and fragrant plants. In our world, herb gardens befitting an Egyptian pharaoh thrive on city fire escapes and suburban decks. No doubt bonsai masters from 8th century China would feel compelled to meditate

A teeming container garden turns a rear entryway into a work of art. Like a flower border in miniature, the interplay of flowers and foliage is constantly changing.

Large-flowered gloxinias can be grown outdoors in the summer, and brought into bloom indoors from late winter to spring.

Pretty pansies in an unexpected pair of planters bring a fun touch to the container garden.

A bougainvillea, grown as bonsai, can be counted upon for vibrant spring color year after year.

Combining different plants in container bouquets is a rewarding ritual of spring. Here purple petunias are planted alongside Russian sage.

all day over a pot-grown azalea in full bloom.

Although container gardening is well documented in tomb paintings dating back to the reign of Ramses II in Egypt over 3,000 years ago, container gardening today is like no other gardening in history. If you delve into books on container gardening written only 20 years ago, you will find that the primary subjects are houseplants in decorative pots. In a very short period of time, container gardening has evolved into a unique outdoor-indoor horticultural art that makes use of a wide range of techniques borrowed from other specialized fields of gardening, from landscape design to kitchen gardening to space-age plant propagation.

CHANGING TO CONTAINERS

The recent growth of the bedding plant industry has played a major role in this story, for all gardening—including growing plants in containers—is faster, simpler and less prone to failure when you can begin with healthy young plants rather than seeds the size of grains of sand. Only 30 years ago, the materials we now take for granted, such as sterile potting mixes, expertly propagated perennials and featherweight plastic pots, simply were not available. No wonder today's gardeners are having so much fun discovering the many ways plants can be enjoyed without ever pushing a shovel into the ground.

Many container gardeners point out that the comparatively low labor requirement of container gardening makes it almost addictive. Heavy digging and weeding are not part of the con-

Recapturing Runaways

SINCE GROWING PLANTS IN CONTAINERS automatically makes them stay put, container gardeners can grow plants that spread so fast that they have been banished from many gardens. Mint is a fine example, for most cultivars are living examples of what is meant by the phrase, "too much of a good thing." They spread like wildfire, and just when you think you have pulled out the last errant sprig, a new crop appears in all the wrong places. This is not a problem in containers, whether the invasive plant in question is variegated vinca vine, morning glory or wily wisteria.

tainer gardening scene, which means that you do not need a strong back to enjoy success when growing plants in pots. In South Carolina, I once visited the home of a practicing physician, confined to a wheelchair, who tended a riotous collection of blue scaevola, pink impatiens and dozens of other plants without ever leaving his deck. In Florida, a blind gardener showed me her container-grown collection of herbs. Each plant she recognized instantly by touch and fragrance. More recently, a retired couple were featured in the lifestyle section of my local newspaper; their yard was packed with summer annuals, not a one of which was grown in the ground. Instead, they grew their petunias and coleus and marigolds in black plastic nursery liners, discarded by a local landscaping service, and hid the pots beneath a thick mulch of pine needles.

The growing popularity of container gardening has also helped us discover many useful new plants, and rediscover many old ones. These days, every spring sees the introduction of new plants and varieties tailor-made for container culture. In 1997, All America Selections, a

In this lush deck garden, a collection of cacti and succulents offers a glimpse of the desert in the middle of a jungle.

Yellow cushion mums bring autumnal highlights to a bed of evergreen shrubs.

Easily grown citrus trees bring triple rewards—fragrant foliage, flowers and delicious fruits.

national organization that helps identify, evaluate and promote outstanding plants, gave awards to two new outstanding container varieties: 'Crystal White' *Zinnia angustifolia* (narrow-leaf zinnia) and 'Gypsy' *Gypsophilia muralis* (annual baby's breath). In 1998, AAS helped a new generation of gardeners rediscover the beauty of up to eight shades of Swiss chard by spotlighting the 'Bright Lights' cultivar. Another organization that promotes stellar plants, called Proven Winners, constantly promotes new plants that quickly become container garden mainstays, including 'Blue Wonder' scaevola, a greatly expanded selection of trailing verbenas and lots of little ground cover plants with intricately variegated leaves.

A narrow courtyard provides ample room for a vast selection of vegetables and flowers, and still leaves open space for outdoor living.

A planting pillar is hidden from view by the lush growth of fuchsia, artemisia and geraniums surrounding a single honeybush (Melianthus major).

THE PAINTERLY PASSION

With so many plants to work with—including dozens that often grow better in containers than when planted in the ground—container gardeners have created a unique new art form. Whether you call them plant compositions or container bouquets, most container gardeners find pleasure in experimenting with innovative plant combinations. If you were to ask a roomful of container gardeners about their favorite plant partnerships, certainly you would hear about several very different approaches. There would be high-contrast color partnerships, such as fragrant purple heliotrope that seems to arise from a foamy sea of white alyssum. There would be three-tiered forms, in which an upright silvery artemisia presides over a court of pert pink petunias and lacy shoots of variegated ivy. There would be adventurous use of texture, in which the glossy leaves of a carefully tended rose are surrounded by ferny pots of pastel achillea. Some compositions attempt to do it all by combining colors, forms and textures, while others make a clear but simple statement with singularly beautiful plants. An amaryllis in full bloom needs no company. The best use of a bushy chartreuse coleus might be to slip it into the background where its main job would be to glow like a giant firefly.

Do not be discouraged if you are a beginning gardener who chokes on botanical names. Even if you do not know a *Salvia* from a *Scilla* now, you will be surprised at how much you learn with each passing growing season. The day

When pot-grown mums and other perennials come into bloom, move them to a highly visible spot.

In containers, a large collection of plants requires little space, as seen with these African violets.

you take your plants home from a garden center, they will be new acquaintances. As you place them in pots, they will become friends. By the end of the season, you will know them as trusted companions, and already be making plans to handle them differently, perhaps partnering them with something new, or perhaps never growing them again. Start small, try to have fun and your plants will teach you

The deliciously fragrant foliage of scented geraniums can be addictive. Different species may smell of apple, lemon, rose or even chocolate.

much of what you need to know.

This book is intended to jump-start the learning process, whether you are a new gardener or an experienced one who has decided to find out what all the fuss is about. First we will spend a couple of chapters on elementary design, the containers themselves and the nuts and bolts of soil and fertilizer. The rest of the book is about plants and what you can do with them in your container garden. There are ideas here for growing more than 200 fine container plants from carrots to clematis. It is up to you to turn these ideas into living works of art.

Chapter 2

※

THE ARTFUL USE OF CONTAINERS

ontainers filled with plants fit in every garden, regardless of its size. Containers provide the only way to garden on apartment terraces or townhouse patios, but plants growing in pots, boxes and baskets bring new possibilities to large gardens, as well. This chapter is about using containers to make your outdoor space more attractive and enjoyable. Whether you hope to grow five or 50 plants in containers, the way to begin is to consider how the entire undertaking can best bring you a happy feeling of satisfaction.

No two gardens are alike because different people want different things from their plants. However, there are proven strategies, borrowed from the field of landscape design, that can provide you with quick answers to at least some of your questions about what to grow and where to grow it.

Difficult sites such as this sloping side yard can become gardens through the use of containers filled with flowers. Annuals and perennials play major roles.

A strong red and green color scheme is carried out in flowers, containers and painted lattice panel.

A concrete pedestal urn filled with flowers becomes an irresistible focal point.

Art knows no boundaries in the container garden, as seen here with flowers, a painted clay pot and cut metal sculpture.

Repeating pots of fountain grass in pedestal planters emphasize a formal style.

CREATING A FORMAL STYLE

If your personal tastes run toward neat orderliness, you will probably be most comfortable with what is known as formal design. In formal landscapes, containers often are arranged symmetrically, so that the picture created by the container garden has a strong feeling of balance. For example, you might place two matching dwarf junipers on either side of your front door, and color up the area with twin hanging baskets of browallia or petunia.

Another strategy that creates a formal feel is to plant several identical containers with the same type of plant, and

Heavy shrubs can be left in place permanently, or moved when needed with the help of a wheeled dolly.

You can change indoor display plants as individual specimens grow into lovely forms, as seen in this lavender plant.

amazingly tailored look, and leaf lettuce and parsley look like green lace.

Container bouquets, in which several very different plants are combined in a single container, can also carry out a formal mood. Tulips and pansies are a classic team that grow with almost military precision, and several cascading

place these in a repetitive pattern to create a strong, rhythmic line. Many formal-minded container gardeners use begonias or impatiens this way, for these plants grow into naturally neat mounds and can adapt to many types of containers. However, you need not grow only flowers. Globe-type basils have an

White flowers, gray gravel and plenty of dusty miller make this soft gray garden glow, day or night.

Miniature pansies and daisies in identical pots provide a neat line of bright color.

In containers, well-dressed trees wear a colorful cover of flowers at their feet.

Personal touches make every container garden unique. Here, ivy topiaries preside over a small tub garden and mixed container bouquets.

plants, including annual lobelia and long-lived English ivy, always look elegant and refined in the company of more upright plants.

IDEAS FOR INFORMAL AREAS

Even if you favor a formal look for the front of your home, you may want to develop your patio, deck or backyard garden with fun and relaxation in mind. Follow your heart in your private retreat, and give in to your dreams of growing

Five species makes a pretty crowd when the players are primrose, pansy, ranunculus, artemisia and tulip.

The gray tones of the birch tree's bark are amplified by silvery sprays of dusty miller.

fragrant, delicious or weird plants, just because you like them.

Informal container gardens need not look messy if they are unified in some way. During the summer, when annuals strut their colors, choose a certain flower each year to help tie your collection of containers into a whole. White petunias are champions at this trick, but depending on how much sun and space you have, you might use a number of other

A wagon full of succulents requires little care, and always makes pleasant company.

white, soft yellow or pale pink flowers as your visual "glue".

To tame down the wildest plant collection imaginable—one in which no two containers are alike—plug away with plants with cool gray foliage such as lamb's-ear, dusty miller or a variety of artemisias. Silvery gray and white seem to go with everything, and the more of it you use, the less your container garden will look like a crazy quilt.

ACCENTING SPECIAL SPACES

With some general notions about style beginning to gel in your mind, zero in on the best places to display your container gardening masterpieces. Entryways are obvious choices, for

Tulips always attract attention and help bring order to a lively spring container garden.

Geranium and white lamium make an elegant entryway combination.

Continuity is the key to this stair-step planting of geraniums and heliotrope. The variegated geranium provides much needed contrast.

Above-Ground Beds

*I*F PLANTING FLOWER BEDS IN your yard is too much work, you can create a nice facsimile using containers. Mow and rake the area, and cover it with a sheet of perforated black plastic mulch or another roll-out material that permits excess water to drip through. Plant low, wide plastic pots with colorful flowers, and place them close together on the unmade bed. Mulch around and between the plants with pine needles to hide the containers.

walkways and doors are the places where we tend to pause and look around to enjoy plants up close. Even if the light exposure is not great right by your door, you can shift containers about so that they occupy that coveted space when they are at their peak of beauty or fragrance.

Is there a window in your home that you look out of every day? Is there a place that is always in view when you wash dishes or sit on your patio? These

Flowers, herbs and foliage plants frame a back door that leads to a small patio and lawn area. The repetition of the pansies helps hold the arrangement together.

Simplicity is always appropriate for entryways, which should feel open, airy and clean.

Symmetry and balance are the hallmarks of this large clay planter filled with amaranthus, nicotiana and lantana.

Safety First

BE CAREFUL WHEN ADORNING walkways and driveways with container plants, for safety should always come first. When placing containers in areas that are often used at night, fill them with white or light-colored plants that are easy to see in the dark.

COLOR AND TEXTURE

In container gardening, you are mixing and matching the colors and textures of plants as well as the colors and textures of containers. Certainly you will know winning combinations when you see them, but a bit of advice here does seem in order. The gray tones of stone and weathered concrete go with everything, and are particularly useful when you are trying to make the most of pink and blue flowers. Good old terra-cotta orange containers are perfectly at home with red or yellow flowers, but may detract from soft pinks.

Instead of trying to follow rigid rules about colors and textures, we container gardeners might use a mental checklist when creating our gardens. Do the colors and textures of the plants flatter each other? Do you have a container that will do the plants justice? Are the plants and the container suitable for the place where

Nasturtiums make a profuse display of hot color. The wheelbarrow is easily moved to make the most of available sunshine.

you plan to put them? This last question may be impossible to answer if you are new to container gardening, for containers vary in their ability to withstand drying sun, freezing cold and other natural elements. You can grow plants in any type of container that can hold soil and water, including old shoes, rusted red wagons or any number of other items. Once bitten by the container gardening bug, you will probably find yourself inspecting all sorts

places are ideal sites for developing focal points with beautiful containers. For example, a large, colorful container bouquet surrounded by other containers that provide contrasting texture, such as a collection of bright annuals accompanied by hostas, becomes an irresistible focal point. When well-placed, tub gardens filled with water plants and a few fish are nothing less than mesmerizing.

Pretty primroses bring new life to an old mud boot.

Smooth-textured cooking pots make perfect petunia planters in a weathered stone fireplace. Lots of colors make the arrangement whimsical and fun.

The weathered wood of an old wheelbarrow is perfect for primroses. During harsh weather, they can be wheeled to a protected spot.

of things before tossing them into the garbage, just in case they might be used to grow a plant. At the same time, proper pots and other purchased containers will likely be your basic equipment year after year. The following gallery of containers summarizes the characteristics of the most popular types available at stores.

High contrast colors make the magic behind this hanging basket. Yellow tuberous begonia and blue lobelia set the stage.

Borage and other herbs thrive in a rusty wagon. Plenty of drainage holes and a gritty soil mixture make the plan work.

White cyclamen grow from a hidden clay pot, slipped inside an old wicker fish creel.

A Gallery of Containers

Good containers come in an endless array of shapes and sizes, with a similar variety of prices. The most versatile containers have at least one drainage hole in the bottom through which excess water can escape. When using containers that have no drainage holes, it is best to grow your plants in a clay or plastic pot that does allow for drainage, and slip it inside the one that lacks a hole, set on a shallow bed of gravel or pebbles.

Terra-cotta pots and planters

Familiar orange clay pots can be found both plain and fancy, in many varied shapes. Terra-cotta containers come in various grades. Those with tags or stamps that indicate Italian origin are made from a very fine clay, and tend to be harder and more moisture retentive than Mexican or American made pottery. Italian terra-cotta also has a slightly satiny patina, compared to a flat, powdery finish on North American products. Expect to pay more for Italian terra-cotta.

Terra-cotta pots are affordable and versatile, but they are prone to crack when the wet soil inside them freezes in winter. North of Zone 7, they are best emptied and stored dry through winter. In warm

Dozens of geraniums in terra cotta pots are ready for summer.

Terra cotta containers come in all shapes and sizes, as well as different grades.

The shape and pattern of this pot work well with a partnership of daffodils and pansies.

The strict form of a clipped Alberta spruce needs no embellishment.

To make special terra cotta containers last, it is best to store them clean and dry through the winter.

Three stacks of clay pots provide height for a pedestal planted with ivy topiary.

A European country motif is played out in a relief pattern of grapes.

The face of the sun would be a good match with blazing summer flowers.

weather, small terra-cotta pots dry out very quickly, but this is less of a problem with containers more than 12 inches wide, or when the pots are used in damp, shady places. And, because terra-cotta containers do drain quickly, they make fine temporary quarters for young plants that are at high risk of developing root rot.

Clay pots and planters

Containers made from white or gray clay, or from multicolored mixtures of white, orange and gray clay, provide interesting variations when arranged in groups with terra-cotta containers. White clay pots usually cost more, and are typically available only in large sizes.

Regardless of color, clay pots tend to crack in freezing winter weather. Weight also can be a problem, for any clay pot larger than 16 inches will be very heavy when filled with damp soil and plants. Clay containers that are glazed on the outside hold water

This stamped repetitive pattern carries the historical feel of ancient pottery.

Depending on placement, these simple fluid lines might suggest water or windblown sand.

The glazing on the outside of this strawberry pot enhances its ability to retain water.

Clay pots break easily when they freeze, but are fine for plants that spend the winter indoors.

Clay strawberry planters work well in partial to full shade, for sun dries them quickly.

Containers for bonsai are usually low and broad, so that the plant's base and surrounding soil are clearly visible.

Because of their stability, containers that are broad at the base are good to use near walkways.

Unusual forms of cacti and succulents fill a flat dish.

Variations in shape, size and materials bring visual interest to the container garden.

When clean and dry, terra cotta containers can be painted with enamel paint.

better than unglazed ones, and they are easier to clean, too. However, always check for the presence of a drainage hole when considering a pot or planter with a ceramic glaze. Adding one later (using a power drill equipped with a masonry bit) can be tricky.

Plastic pots and planters

Lightweight plastic pots and planters are a great value. Many come with pop-off trays that catch drainage water, and the color range is huge. Most gardeners stick with the three standard colors intended to mimic clay and ceramic—sandy white, terra-cotta orange and forest green. Admittedly, there is something undeniably tacky about a pink plastic Grecian urn, but plastic window box liners and featherweight

Indoors or out, plastic pots can easily pass for terra cotta.

Plenty of open space between containers helps to lighten the heavy presence of concrete and muscular tree limbs.

Lightweight black plastic pots absorb solar heat, retain soil moisture and hold up well to repeated freezing and thawing.

Versatile plastic pots may be tucked into baskets, or wrapped in paper, cloth or strips of fabric wallcovering.

Between seasons, plastic pots are perfect for a working nursery area.

Primroses grow in plastic pots hidden inside white ceramic ones.

tree-sized planters (for under $15) will eventually win you over.

Even the best quality plastic does not last forever. After about three years of winter cold and summer heat, expect plastic con-tainers to become some-what brittle. On the plus side, plastic containers hold moisture very well, and they weigh next to nothing.

Fiberglass pots and planters

The newest types of plant containers, made from molded fiberglass foam, offer the look of terra-cotta at a fraction of the weight. Most show decorative relief patterns on the outside. They can be made even more attractive by brushing lightly with white or gray latex paint, and then immed-iately wiping it off so that the paint remains faintly imbedded in the pattern's crevices.

Fiberglass containers hold up beautifully to all types of weather, and take years to show signs of strain. They are widely available as elongated boxes and pots, but hard to find in more interesting shapes. In addition to the most common terra-cotta color, you may find some of a sandy gray color intended to mimic concrete or stone.

Pressed paper planters are ideal for short-lived annuals such as these lemon-yellow zinnias.

Etched with lichens, old stone planters are art pieces by themselves.

Concrete planters

The massive weight of concrete planters makes them almost permanent fix-tures in the container garden. They are a classic way to accent entry gates, and they work well as permanent focal points where garden paths cross. Because of their extreme weight, they are best placed on stone or earth surfaces rather than decks or sus-

Is it stone, concrete, plastic or fiberglass? You may need to tap it to be certain.

This hypertufa trough is made by molding a concrete-peat mixture between cardboard boxes.

pended terraces. The tonnage of concrete is an asset if you are worried about thieves, and concrete is excellent for complementing garden statuary.

Drainage can be a problem with flat-bottomed concrete planters, so look for specimens with feet that hold them aloft. Large concrete pedestal urns usually have an iron connecting pipe that serves as a drainage hole.

Stone planters

These are rare in the United States, and stone pots and boxes offered by upscale garden centers are usually hand-made, with price tags starting at around $250.

The balance and symmetry of this composition match the container perfectly.

Long popular in Europe because they positively breathe history, stone planters are awesome when well situated and filled with beautiful plants.

Their expense aside, stone planters are always large, and often weigh more than 70 pounds. If you buy one, make arrangements for

its installation. If the planter does not have feet that hold it above the ground, prepare a level platform of color-coordinated brick or stone to allow at least one inch of free space underneath for drainage.

Wood boxes and planters

Unless it is stained or painted, any type of wood container used outdoors will eventually weather to gray. Inexpensive pine or poplar boxes will last longer if treated with a waterseal product every other year, while cedar and redwood require less maintenance. If you build your own wood boxes, use screws rather

Herbs grow happily in wood boxes securely attached to a terrace rail.

A planter with its own window—a brilliant twist for a plain black box.

To help them last, treat wood planters with a sealant before using them.

A decorative stone planter needs little embellishment.

Stone troughs are traditional containers for alpine plants.

To use a wood box to display special plants, simply place the pot inside.

Inexpensive and light, white plastic urns make good containers for showy foliage plants such as caladiums.

Containers can make small lawns come in all shapes and sizes.

than nails to hold the corners together. Before planting a large wood box with a tree or shrub, install rollers on its base to make it easy to move around. Most container gardeners use plastic pots or plastic window box liners inside their wood planters.

Treated wood containers are not good choices for growing fruits and vegetables. Unless the planters are holding plants that will grow indoors through winter, they are customarily cleaned and stored dry through the winter. Painted boxes usually need repainting every two or three years.

Brass and copper planters

Planters made from thin brass or copper are ideal for showcasing refined flowers. They work best when used indoors or on protected porches and patios, where they are sheltered from weather. Slip plastic pots inside brass or copper ones, for the metal containers usually lack drainage holes, and constant moisture takes a heavy toll on metal seams.

Store brass or copper planters in a cool, dry place when you are not using them. These types of planters are more decorative than practical. However, a nice brass planter placed in the center of your patio table may be the perfect place to put potted flowers or herbs when they are in perfect condition.

Retired from the hearth and barn, these containers are put back into service.

A sphagnum moss lining flatters a simply pansy planter.

The neighbors will never be bothered by this bird's calls.

Plain upright containers often benefit from the addition of cascading plants.

A wood watering trough is a lovely annual garden, all by itself.

Painted metal baskets are mounted below eye level for easy viewing.

Half barrels

For $20 to $30, you can buy half barrels recycled from the brewing of whiskey or wine, or new planters made from cedar and shaped like half barrels. These can be planted with large container bouquets, vegetables, shrubs or trees, or you can use them for growing a container water garden.

If you want a deep water garden that can accomodate a few fish, you will also need an aquarium-grade liner, available where pond supplies are sold. Many gar-

A small half barrel planted with tuberous begonias.

den centers sell drop-in plastic liners for the tops of half barrels that are about 7 inches deep—just right for many aquatic plants, but too shallow for fish.

Metal hanging baskets

Round hanging baskets made from painted steel—or iron hayrack planters that hang from flat walls or fences—will last for decades if given proper care. Either type of container requires the use of a sheet-type liner made from moss or coconut fiber. To install plants in the sides or bottom of these containers, you slit the liners with a sharp knife

Metal hayrack planters, lined with sheets made from coconut fibers.

and slip the plants in through these cuts.

After a couple of seasons of use, look for small rust spots. After sanding off the rust, paint steel baskets or racks with a rust retardant paint. Flat black rust retardant paint is preferred for cast iron. To reduce rusting, store metal planters in a dry place through the winter.

Grow bags

Some stores sell perforated plastic bags filled with potting soil, ready for planting. Simply open up

Wire baskets lined with sphagnum moss hold a variety of bedding begonias.

Feathery pampas grass in a half barrel accents a mailbox.

You can use grow bags to plant an instant garden almost anywhere. They can be laid on the ground or placed on tables or benches.

The unusual texture of an aluminum pail works well with a black iron hanger.

Sturdy yet beautiful, a custom made iron pot holder looks like a tree.

the planting holes, pop in your seeds and plants and add water. In a pinch, you can even use 20 pound bags of inexpensive potting soil to grow plants from cucumbers to coleus. Make several drainage holes in the side of the bag that will be on the ground before dampening

and planting it, and see if you can find a wood packing pallet to put under the bag to make sure excess water can drain off easily. Grow bags look best when planted with plants that sprawl or vine to cover this rather primitive type of container.

Special hanging hardware

You can adorn deck railings or a wood privacy fence with plants by using special hardware made for this purpose. Painted metal pot holders that hook over the top of a fence are widely available, along with others

that are screwed into the fence. Hook-type hangers for deck railings are fine if the deck is close to the ground. However, when attaching boxes or planters to high balconies, look for hanging hardware that can be securely screwed onto the railing.

The lush growth of tuberous begonias and mini-pansies hides wall-mounted baskets.

A variety of baskets and pots have been used to create a tropical outdoor room.

CONTAINER COLORS

Choosing the right color container for plants can make a big difference in how the plants look and how well they grow. Black or dark green containers collect solar heat, which makes them a good choice for growing tomatoes, cannas or other warm-natured plants in a cool climate. However, in hot summer areas, black pots may heat up so much that the plants' roots cook on hot days. Shielding black pots with aluminum foil is an easy way to keep the roots inside from overheating during hot summer weather.

In comparison, white, gray or other light-colored containers reflect solar rays, so they do a good job of helping keep plant roots cool. However, do keep in mind that dense concrete or thick terra-cotta planters set in full sun will hold on to the day's heat well into evening, the same way a sidewalk remains warm long after the sun has set.

SHAPES AND SIZES

In any container garden, there are places for many different types of containers. Tall, narrow containers such as terra-cotta strawberry planters tend to heat up and dry out quickly, which makes them an excellent choice for sedums and other succulents, but far from ideal for impatiens and other plants that need continuous moisture. Very small pots also dry out fast, yet they, too, have a place in your collection of containers. When propagating stem cuttings (see page 74) or babying small plants that have skimpy root systems, it is best to keep them in smallish containers until they develop more substantial roots. If you set a tiny plant in a large container, there is an increased risk that the plant may develop a problem with root rot, caused by a number of different soil-dwelling fungi. However, if you situate small plants in small, clean containers and move them to roomier quarters later on, they are more likely to enjoy steady growth free of disease problems.

You might notice something missing in your container garden, and it is likely to be height. Occasional pillars or strongly upright plants are welcome sights in the container garden, for they create a new dimension that greatly amplifies visual interest. Vertical accents also help keep plants and containers in appropriate scale. Large containers planted with low plants often look huge, but including some taller, vertical plants fixes this problem and ensures that the plants, rather than the container, are the stars of the show.

In the next chapter, you will find extensive information on potting soils, fertilizers and working with container-grown plants in different types of climates. The plant profiles, which appear later on in this book, will usually suggest an appropriate container size, and occasionally a container material, as well. Unlike gardeners who grow all of their plants in the ground, container gardeners have the advantage of being able to tightly control their plants' soil, light exposure, nutrients and growing habits. It is that element of control that makes container gardens uniquely beautiful, productive and fun to grow.

Low dishes are well suited to plants that do not require constant moisture.

Painting containers can help to give them a weathered appearance.

Container gardens grow best when the containers are chosen to meet the needs of each plant.

Plants that have a spillover habit put the pockets of strawberry jars to good use.

Chapter 3

※

THE BASICS OF CONTAINER GARDENING

W hen plants are grown in containers, they are much more dependent on the care we give them than are plants that grow in the ground. Sunlight, soil, food and water are entirely within our control, and that's both an asset and an affliction. On the positive side, this extreme degree of control makes it possible for us to stretch seasonal limits, experiment with plants that require special soil, temperature or light conditions, or grow plants close together in artistic looking colonies. The disadvantage is that container gardens will not survive long if neglected. In this chapter, you will learn about special container gardening techniques and materials that can help make your pot-grown plants as self-sufficient as possible. At the same time, perhaps the most basic aspect of container gardening is that the gardener must be prepared to spend a few min-

Selecting the best exposure for plants is as important as soil, water and nutrients.

Place feet, bricks or stones beneath pots to promote excellent drainage.

utes each day making sure every plant is content.

DRAINAGE IS ESSENTIAL

Drainage is to container gardening as location is to real estate. It's everything. You can do everything else wrong—forget to fertilize your pansies, stick sun lovers such as tomatoes in shady corners or overwater drought-tolerant flowers such as coreopsis—and your plants will survive if the containers have good drainage. But try to grow plants in pots with poor drainage, and the roots will begin to suffer immediately, and the plants will eventually die.

Most pots have a single drainage hole in the center of the bottom, while others have four or five holes around the bottom edges of the pots. Those with more numerous drainage holes usually drain faster than pots with single holes. So, you might grow plants that need a lot of moisture, such as impatiens or azalea, in pots with only one drainage hole, and use your fastest draining pots for plants that prefer dry soil, such as artemisia or thyme.

Some plastic pots that appear to have no holes actually have them. Look closely at their bottoms for perforated circles. Some will bear the inscription: *Press here.* Push the tip of a table knife or screwdriver against the perforation and press. A plastic plug will fall away, and a drainage hole will be created. There are usually four or five perforations in a rectangular plastic window box liner, and all should be pushed out for the best drainage.

Many plastic pots include trays that snap onto the bottom of the pot. These trays catch the water that seeps out through the pots' drainage holes, which eliminates a lot of dripping around your deck or patio. At the same time, having those trays constantly full of water stops the drainage process. When using containers with trays, either water just enough so that very little excess water drains out, or water as heavily as you wish and then come back after 45 minutes or so and tip the pots to pour out the standing water in the trays.

RAISING CONTAINERS

In addition to using containers that allow water to escape through holes in their bottoms, you must place containers so that the drainage holes are not blocked.

Raise your containers so that the water has somewhere to go. Also, because most container gardening takes place on concrete patios or wooden porches or decks, avoiding permanent stains from moist containers is important. A constantly wet clay pot will imprint a dark ring quickly on most surfaces.

Brick, stones and clay pot feet can be used to raise containers a minimum of one half inch above the ground. Two inches is better, especially in damp climates. Ornate terra-cotta and concrete pot feet are available at garden centers and through mail order catalogs, too. Among the many styles available, you can find ones to complement most any decorative container. You can even use pieces of pressure-treated lumber if you like, but they tend to dry slowly and may attract slugs or other unwanted pests, and shouldn't be used for growing fruits or vegetables.

If you prefer, you can prepare a bed for your container garden by building a shallow wood frame and filling it with at least one inch of pebbles or small stones. Pots can be set directly atop this bed, for the excess water will drain easily through the pebbles.

PRETTY POTS WITHOUT HOLES

Instead of trying to drill drainage holes in them, some large glazed ceramic pots, elaborately surfaced concrete urns and metal containers are best used as cache pots. A cache pot is one that is utilized as decorative sleeve for another pot or pots. This is the best thing to do with very beautiful pots that might be ruined if you tried to add holes to them, or metal pots that would quickly rust or discolor if they were constantly exposed to moist soil.

Of course, you do not actually grow a plant in a cache pot. Instead, wait until special plants are nearing their peak of perfection, and then use your loveliest containers to display them. For example,

Use decorative ceramic planters to showcase beautiful plants. This camellia is actually growing in a plastic pot.

A hammer and large nail are all you need to add drainage holes to an aluminum tub.

you might nurture a chrysanthemum all summer in a dirty plastic pot, and then slip it into a Chinese ceramic urn just as the buds begin to open. If needed, use dry sphagnum moss to hide the top of the container from view. Several small pots can be grouped in a cache pot, too, using the same techniques.

But there is an important intermediate step. To make sure your plant enjoys good drainage inside the cache pot, place two inches of clean pea gravel or crushed rock in the bottom of the cache pot, beneath the plant. When keeping plants in cache pots, water them carefully by dribbling water into the inner pots. Check for standing water in the bottom of the cache pot, and drain it off if

needed by tilting the container on its side. Because of their lack of drainage, place cache pots where they are sheltered from rain when using them outdoors.

SOIL FOR CONTAINERS

The ideal container soil should be loose and porous so that water, fertilizer and air can move quickly to the plants' roots. Water should drain rapidly and enough soil should be present to hold moisture, fertilizer and air. Materials that make up the soil should be free of soil-borne diseases and weed seeds. No matter how good your garden soil may be, it will not meet these requirements. Besides, the ability of the soil to actually provide plant nutrients is of minor

Quality packaged potting soils are formulated to meet the needs of most plants.

hard crust over germinating seeds, and are free of the fungi that often cause young seedlings to rot.

Other potting soils that contain loam (real soil) and composted manure tend to be heavier and can compact easily in containers. Drainage is usually slower in soil-based mixtures, because soil holds water longer than milled peat moss. However, heavy soil-based mixtures are preferred for some plants. Like soilless mixes, bags of loam or potting soil are readily available at garden centers. They cost less than premium quality soilless mixtures.

MAKING YOUR OWN MIXES

Although bagged soilless mix is easy to find and meets the needs of almost any plant you might grow in a container, you may want to create special mixtures for certain plants. For example, some herbs grow better in a sandy mixture, while shrubs and trees may prefer an extra dose of peat moss or soil around their roots. Many container gardeners keep several soil amendments on hand to mix with their favorite packaged products, or with soil dug from the ground. A list of the most useful soil amendments follows, along how you might use them in your container garden.

In soil mixing lingo, the phrase "equal parts" means equal parts in volume, which can be measured in cups, pints, coffee cans or buckets. For example, a mixture of equal parts peat moss, sand and vermiculite would contain an equal

importance when you are growing plants in containers. Any nutrients present in the soil are leached out quickly from frequent watering. The potting soil you use in your container garden is best thought of as a medium that provides the kind of texture plants like. We will talk about fertilizer a little later in this chapter.

For most plants, the first choice in potting soil is a packaged sterile soilless mix, also called professional potting mix or premium quality potting soil. These products, made of milled (finely shredded) peat moss, vermiculite or perlite, sand and perhaps shredded bark or compost, are available at garden centers and discount stores. These mixtures are sterilized so they are free of fungi and

weed seeds. Even if you opt to use a homemade potting soil for some of your plants, always use a sterile soilless mix for starting seeds. They do not form a

Sterilizing Potting Soil

HIGH QUALITY SOILLESS MIXES ARE STERILIZED before they are packaged, but fungi and bacteria quickly move in after the bag is opened. As long as the bag is kept in a dry place, contamination by microorganisms need not be a serious worry. However, if the mixture was opened the previous year and was dampened, it is a good idea to sterilize it before using it to grow seedlings or tender young plants. To sterilize any soil, place it in a metal or glass pan, sprinkle lightly with water to dampen it, and cover tightly with foil. Place it in a 200°F oven for at least one hour, so that the accumulated steam can kill any life forms present in the soil. Allow the soil to cool completely before using it. If you make your own soil from a variety of materials, keep a large foil pan with your gardening supplies for sterilizing small batches used to plant seeds.

measure of each of these ingredients. If you like tinkering with custom soil mixtures, keep several large tin cans in your potting area for scooping up various materials.

UNDERSTANDING SOIL pH

Soilless mix and bagged potting soil usually are neutral in terms of pH, a measure of acidity versus alkalinity. Most plants like near neutral soil that is neither acid or alkaline. The scale that measures pH runs from 0 to 14, the neutral point being 7. Anything less than 7 is acidic, and any number higher is alkaline. Most commercial soil blends register between 6.5 and 7.5 on the pH scale. There are a few plants that require either acid or alkaline soil. It's easy to adjust the pH of soilless mix to accommodate them.

Acid lovers such as blueberries and azaleas need a pH of about 5.5. Extra peat moss incorporated into soil mixes will lower the pH, as will using a fertilizer formulated for acid-loving plants (such as aluminum sulfate). For perennial plants that remain in the same container year after year, the best way to maintain a pH of about 5.5 is to incorporate a small amount of sulfur into the soil every spring. Garden sulfur is sold in five pound sacks in nurseries. Invest in a pH meter or buy an inexpensive soil test kit that measures pH before adding sulfur to container soil, and follow the directions on the package for the amount to add to each container.

Other plants such as rosemary and lavender grow best in alkaline soil, which is often called limey soil. Ground limestone, which is simply referred to as lime, is the best way to raise the pH to about 7.5. Lime is also sold in four or five pound bags or boxes at garden centers. A quarter cup or less mixed well into container soil will do the job. Again, test for pH and then follow package instructions for the amount to add. Lime should also be applied every spring to the soil of perennials that remain in the same container in order to maintain a high pH.

Ten Useful Soil Amendments

● Bark is the outer, corky layer of trees that is dried and chunked or shredded. Most packaged bark is pine bark, a by-product of the lumber industry. It is usually quite acidic, and rarely makes a good addition to potting mixtures. However, shredded bark is a fine mulch material to place atop the soil in containers planted with trees, shrubs or large perennials.

● Compost can be made from any plant material that is thoroughly rotted. Products in bags labeled as compost are highly variable in content. Gardeners who keep a compost bin or heap for composting vegetable wastes from the kitchen sometimes add the finished product to potting mixtures for some plants, for compost is often a good source of minor nutrients.

● Humus is kind of a catch-all word for organic matter, and garden centers often sell products in bags that are labeled as humus. Rotted manure, leaf mold and compost all are forms of humus.

● Loam is high quality soil that contains large amounts of organic material, or humus. Good loam is rich in naturally occurring nutrients, and useful for creating soil-based potting mixtures.

● Manure sold in bags has almost always been processed two ways. First it is composted in combination with straw, sawdust or other materials, and then it is dried and pulverized. Products sold in bags labeled as manure are highly variable in content, so try several products if you intend to add packaged manure to potting mixtures. Mix it in very well. Processed manure is most useful as an addition to pots in which vegetables are being grown.

● Peat moss is a material taken from bogs in arctic areas. It is sold dried, in blocks, and must be fluffed up and dampened before it is used. Peat moss is naturally acidic. Although lacking in plant nutrients, many fungi that cause plant diseases are unable to grow in peat moss. However, its greatest asset is its ability to absorb water while creating a soft texture that plant roots can penetrate easily. To use peat moss, remove a portion of dry material from the package and dampen it before measuring. Store the rest dry until you need it.

● Sphagnum peat moss is long, somewhat stringy pieces of peat moss that have not been shredded. Sphagnum peat moss is useful for lining baskets or dressing the tops of container grown plants. It is not suitable for mixing with other ingredients to create planting mixtures.

● Perlite is included in many soilless blends, or you can buy it by the bag and mix it with your own soil mixtures. The individual particles, which look like tiny bits of popcorn, are popped chips of volcanic ash. Perlite adds volume to mixtures without adding weight, improves drainage immensely and does not host plant diseases.

● Sand drains very fast and does not hold moisture well, which is exactly what some plants prefer. You can buy 40 or 50 pound sacks of clean sand at builder's supply centers or places that sell children's sand boxes. Bagged sand has been washed and sterilized. Beach sand is not suitable unless it has been thoroughly washed to remove salts.

● Vermiculite is used just like perlite in soilless mixtures. Vermiculite is mica rock that has been heated until it explodes to form lightweight pellets that hold water better than a sponge.

WATERING WISDOM

Plants need a constant supply of water, but they do not want to soak all the time. When roots sit in too much water, they rot and the plants die. Soilless mixes that drain readily prevent problems caused by overwatering, but only you can fill up the watering can or turn on the faucet.

How Much Soil Do You Need?

MANY BRANDS OF POTTING SOIL ARE SOLD by volume measured in quarts. With other brands, the label only states weight, such as 20 or 40 pounds. To make matters more confusing, pots are often measured according to their diameter, though some are measured in quarts or gallons. To estimate how much soil mix to buy or make to fill various sizes of containers, use the following table. If a brand you like is measured by weight rather than volume, compare the size and weight of the bag to another brand that does include volume measurement on its label.

Pot Size	Volume of Soil Held
4 inches	½ quart or two cups
6 inches	1½ quarts
8 inches	6 quarts
10 inches	10 quarts
12 inches	14 quarts
14 inches	18 quarts
16 inches	22 quarts
20 inches	28 quarts
24 inches	36 quarts
30 inches	72 quarts
36 inches	96 quarts

In container gardening, your goal is to supply enough water to keep the soil evenly moist. Soil that has a damp feel when touched, and that looks dark at the surface is evenly moist. Water should not puddle or stand on the container surface for more than a few seconds. Soil should not feel powdery and dry when fingered, either.

To keep soil evenly moist, it may be necessary to water every day during summer months, and even twice a day in very hot weather. But there are no hard and fast rules, for how often you water depends on the weather, the size of the container, the type of material from which it is made, the potting mixture inside and the density of the plants' roots. To water properly, you must check your plants every day. While checking and watering, you will see small problems before they become major ones, and experience the joys of flowers opening their petals and vegetables ripening.

Do keep in mind that the larger the plant, the more water it consumes. When a plant becomes so large that the pot is filled with roots and the stems and leaves form a heavy canopy, you may need to water it more than once a day.

HOW TO WATER

Each container should receive enough water to moisten all of the soil and roots inside. Dousing the plant with water once may not do the trick. Instead, you must water, go on to other plants, and then water them all a second time. If the soil inside the pots has become extremely dry, it may be necessary to go back a third time, for water tends to run off of dry soil faster than it can be absorbed. Soil that is already slightly moist is easier to water than soil that has become very dry.

Try to water as early in the day as possible to give plant foliage time to dry in the sun. Fungal diseases are much more likely to spread on wet leaves than on dry ones. If you have no choice but to water in the evening, try not to dampen the foliage. Aim water directly at the soil at low pressure, so water doesn't splash up on leaves. Mulching the soil in containers will help to prevent splash-ups, too.

You often will be adding fertilizer to the water you give to your plants. If you have a number of plants to feed and water, it is often simplest to keep a supply of plastic milk jugs or small watering

A spray nozzle attached to a garden hose saves time if you have numerous plants to water.

In hot weather, large plants may need thorough soakings twice a day. Water-soluble fertilizers are easily added to a watering can.

cans handy for mixing and dispensing fertilizer. At other times, a fine spray from a hose is a fast and easy way to water a large collection of containers. Use a bubbler or spray wand attached to the hose end to water plants gently yet thoroughly. Be careful when turning on the hose on hot days, and let the water run for minute before you start watering your plants. Otherwise, you might injure plants with the surprisingly hot water in the hose.

GAUGING SOIL MOISTURE

Plants, soil and even the containers will give you signs of water need. Heed them.

Plant

Wilting leaves indicate that plants are stressed for water. Check the soil for moisture content and water immediately. Just before they wilt, plant leaves often turn a lighter, blue-green color to indicate they need water. On very hot days, plants may wilt for a few hours because their leaves lose more water from evaporation than plant roots can replace. If your plants are showing this symptom of stress every day, move them to partial shade until the hot weather passes.

Soil

To best way to tell if a container needs water is to push your index finger into the soil up to the second joint, which is approximately two inches in depth. If your fingertip detects dry soil, the container needs water.

Container

The lighter the container, the less water it contains. Pick up or tilt small and

Watering Parched Pots

*I*F THE SOIL IN A CONTAINER HAS BEEN ALLOWED to dry out completely, use these tricks to remoisten them all the way through. If the containers are small enough to carry, set them in a large tub of water for 30 minutes. Hanging baskets and pots under ten inches wide respond well to this treatment. With larger containers, poke a number of holes in the soil surface with an ice pick or sharp stick. Set a hose near the plant base and let it trickle very slowly for an hour. If your entire container collection becomes dry as a bone, a sprinkler is the best solution.

medium sized pots when they are thoroughly dampened and use the feel as a reference point. If you suspect a pot or window box is dry, lift it and gauge the difference in weight.

DRIP WATERING SYSTEMS

If you don't have the time or inclination to water your container garden by hand every day, consider setting up an automatic watering system. The least expensive way to automate watering is to use a low-pressure soaker hose that is controlled by a programmable timer box at the faucet. Group your containers close together and weave the soaker hose through the pots and tubs. Assuming you have correctly adjusted the water flow so that water barely drips through the soaker hose, set the watering time for 60 to 75 minutes early in the morning. Some water will be wasted as it falls to the ground between containers, but if you water early, puddles will dry up by

Drip hoses threaded through large pots save time and make very efficient use of water.

noon. This easy system works well if all your containers need watering every day.

More sophisticated automated systems that employ adjustable drip emitters are available, too. Again, a programmable timer box is attached to the faucet and a central water hose is run from it. From the central hose, drip tubing fans out to every container. Each of these tubes has an emitter or miniature sprinkler head attached.

Emitters can be adjusted for various flows and water patterns. If a pot requires much less water than its neighbors, an emitter can be set for little or no water flow. There are also emitters that throw a high and wide spray to cover foliage, in the case of plants that require high humidity and wet soil. Emitters that give off a gentle spray also do a better job of dampening all of the soil in plant containers.

Another way to automatically water containers is to use wicks and drip pans. This is an inexpensive system for plants that like humidity and for gardeners who can't check their plants every day. Drip pans require filling only once or twice a week.

Purchase cotton cording (at a fabric store) that is at least a quarter inch in diameter. Cut into lengths equal to the depth of the container plus another ten inches. Before filling the container with soil, run the cord through the drainage hole and tie slip knots in the cord on either side of the drainage hole to prevent movement. Fill the container with dampened soil and then set in plants. Make sure the cord is positioned near the middle of the container and at least six inches sticks out the drainage hole. For large tubs that have more than one drainage hole, thread a cord through each one.

Shallow dishpans, plant saucers and even small children's wading pools can be used for drip pans. Fill them with two to three inches of water. Elevate containers on bricks or rocks so that they are an inch above the water level. Moisten the cotton cords and place them in the water. Each one will act like a wick and continually take up water as the soil in its

container dries. Water in the drip pans should be replaced as needed, depending on the climate and season, usually once or twice a week.

MINERAL AND SALT BUILD-UP

City water supplies and well water often contain minerals and salts that can build up in container soil quickly. After weeks of daily watering and numerous applications of fertilizer (they leave behind salts, too), soils collect these compounds within their air pockets, on the soil's surface, and often on the outside of clay pots. Mineral and salt residue is usually chalky and white. Many of these residues are harmful to plants and others affect the pH of the soil.

You can correct this problem by washing out the soil without removing the plants from their containers. This operation, called leaching, is a cinch. To leach a pot, drench the soil and continue applying a steady stream of water until it freely runs out of the container bottom for at least two minutes. If plants are actively growing, fertilize the container after leaching.

In areas where the water supply is high in minerals or in cities that use salts to soften their municipal water supply, leaching may be necessary every month. In these problem water areas, you can tell when a container needs leaching, because plants will lose vigor and appear pale. Leach before this happens.

Where water quality is not a problem, plan on leaching a container in mid-season and at the end of the growing season if it will be taken indoors for winter. Also, indoor plants and those that overwinter inside should be leached in early spring or when placed outdoors again. To remove salt and mineral buildup from empty pots, scrub them with vinegar and then rinse well.

FERTILIZER FOR CONTAINER GARDENS

Unless you're a chemist, fertilizer terms can be a foreign language. Designations such as N-P-K may mean nothing to you, but they are important when it

Encapsulated time-release fertilizers slowly leach out nutrients each time you water your plants.

ORGANIC AND SYNTHETIC FERTILIZERS

Whether to use organic fertilizers or synthetic chemical compounds is a personal choice, and you do not have to be absolutely loyal to one type or the other. Organic fertilizers are derived from living organisms such as plants and animals, or are mined from naturally occurring mineral deposits. Synthetic fertilizers consist of man-made chemical salts or salt blends and mined minerals.

Many gardening experts recommend using a combination of the two fertilizer types, for each type brings special benefits to the container garden. Organic fertilizers often offer a banquet of micronutrients, while chemical fertilizers excel when it comes to providing the major nutrients quickly and effectively. Gardeners may choose fertilizer types based on the type of plant being grown as well. Edible plants, for example, may taste better if they are fed an organic diet rich in micronutrients. Annual flowers, in comparison, often perform best when fed a steady diet of a balanced chemical blend.

The argument that synthetic fertilizers are more convenient than organic fertilizers is now obsolete. These days, both types of fertilizers can be purchased in powder or liquid concentrates that can be quickly mixed with water and fed to plants. Or you can choose pelleted or encapsulated fertilizers, both organic and synthetic, that slowly release their nutrients each time the plants are watered.

HOW AND WHAT TO FEED PLANTS

In your container garden, you will probably use three types of fertilizer: concentrated liquids or powders that are mixed with water, time-release fertilizers that are mixed with the soil before plants are set in the containers and granular fertilizers for providing extra nutrients to plants that are left in the same containers year after year. Each is applied to plants in a different manner, and all have their uses in container gardening.

comes to selecting the proper fertilizer for your plants. Here's a quick primer on fertilizer lingo that will prepare you to make smart fertilizer choices.

N-P-K

All fertilizers are made up of three main chemical elements: nitrogen (N), phosphorous (P) and potassium (K). All are essential for plant development. The three numbers with hyphens between them on all fertilizer labels, such as 10-10-10, indicate the relative abundance of each chemical element in the fertilizer. Every fertilizer is labeled in this manner: nitrogen first, phosphorous second and potassium last.

Nitrogen

Plants need nitrogen for all of their growth processes. It is the most important type of fertilizer plants need to grow bushy and strong. When plants are grown in containers, the nitrogen supply must be constant. Slow growth and yellowish leaves are the most common symptoms of nitrogen deficiency. Too much nitrogen leads to unusually dark green leaf color, and more leaves and stems than flowers and fruit. A few plants, including ferns, are easily damaged from heavy doses of nitrogen.

Phosphorous

This is often referred to as the flowering fertilizer, for adequate phosphorous is essential for bloom formation. All plants need it for root development, too. The nutrient is abundant in heavy soils that contain lots of clay.

Potassium

Potash is another name for this chemical. Plants rarely need huge amounts of potassium, but it is an essential nutrient for all plant functions. Root crops such as carrots are big potassium users.

Micronutrients

Plants need many other nutrients in minute or micro amounts for plant health. These include calcium, magnesium, sulfur, iron, manganese, zinc, boron, copper, molybdenum and chlorine. The first three micronutrients are just as important to plant growth as the major three, nitrogen, phosphorous and potassium. For example, magnesium is necessary for photosynthesis, the process plants use to create their own energy from light. Look for commercial fertilizers that list micronutrients after the N-P-K marking. Animal manures, compost, seaweed and rock dusts are good organic sources of micronutrients.

Feeding the Leaves

THE BASIC EQUIPMENT PLANTS use to take up nutrients are their roots, but they can also take up fertilizer through their leaves. This process, called foliar feeding, is especially beneficial to plants that are seriously deficient in either major or minor nutrients. Any fertilizer that can be mixed with water can be applied to plant leaves, but because they are so rich in micronutrients, the best choices are organic fish emulsion-seaweed blends. Regardless of what type of fertilizer you try as a foliar application, never apply any liquid substance to plant leaves when the temperature is above 90°F, or in the middle of a bright, sunny day. The newly applied fertilizer will burn leaves. Do your spraying and drenching in the morning, instead.

Concentrated liquids and powders are the most popular choices among container gardeners. You can choose synthetic formulas, such as Miracle-Gro, Shultz or several other name brands, or use organic concentrates such as Roots (a brand name available in several different formulations), fish emulsion or concentrates made from fish emulsion and seaweed extracts. To use any of these concentrates, mix as much as you will use according to label directions, and pour them over the soil in the containers. When feeding young seedlings, it is best to make the mixture a weak one. In fact, some container gardeners routinely feed their plants with a weak fertilizer solution, and include the fertilizer in the water nearly every time they water. The important thing is to not make the mixture too strong, for this could damage plant roots.

Time-release fertilizers are coated pellets of fertilizer that gradually dissolve each time you water. Most brands of synthetic time-release fertilizer (such as Osmocote and Sta-Green, to name only two) will gradually release nutrients for at least three to nine months, depending on the product. Look for products that list both N-P-K and micronutrients on their label. Because they break down gradually in the soil over a three to four month period, organic fertilizers are time-release by their very nature. The best choices for container gardeners are organic fertilizer blends made from several ingredients, including fish meal, feather meal, rock fertilizers and sometimes manures. If you cannot find granular organic fertilizers locally, you can order them through many mail order sources.

Whether you choose synthetic or organic, the best way to use time-release fertilizer is to combine it with soilless potting mix at planting time. Read the label on the product to find out how much to use, and take care to mix the fertilizer in very well. When used this way, it may not be necessary to add fertilizer to the water until you see signs that your plants are in need of extra nutrients. Time-release fertilizers can also fill this need. Simply scatter a small amount over the soil surface and scratch in with a table fork. As you water, the fertilizer will gradually dissolve and percolate into the soil around the plant's roots.

Granular fertilizer usually comes in large bags of five pounds or more. It is very inexpensive. Common granular synthetic fertilizers such as 10–10–10, which is used widely for lawns, fruit trees and vegetables gardens, also can be used with container plants. However, granular fertilizers that include micro-nutrients are usually better. Unlike time-release fertilizer, granular fertilizer dissolves very quickly. After about a dozen good drenchings, any granular fertilizer you mix into the soil at planting time will be used up or leached away. After that, you can switch to a liquid fertilizer or scratch in some more granular fertilizer. To apply granular fertilizer to established container plants, sprinkle the granules evenly over the soil surface, and use a table fork to mix it into the top inch of soil. Water very well after applying a booster feeding of granular fertilizer.

EXCELLENT EXPOSURES

In every yard and on every patio, deck, porch and balcony there are microclimates, which are subtly different from the overall climate of town or state in which you reside. Microclimates are created by shade, sun, wind and the radiated heat from walls, windows or hard concrete surfaces. These factors either heat or cool the air within a small area and create a microclimate that differs from the rest of the yard or patio or even porch. Finding and using the microclimates in your container gardening area is a special skill you will develop over time as you get to know your plants and your place on an intimate level.

For example, imagine a patio garden in Oklahoma City, which is in Zone 7. The first fall frost comes around November 5. The patio faces south, and is protected from cold northerly winds by a wood privacy fence. A thermometer on the patio will register as much as 10 degrees higher than one in the middle of the yard on autumn nights. Near the south-facing brick wall of the patio, the temperature difference may be as much as 20 degrees. Here is a microclimate in which containers can be sheltered when a freeze threatens. In a sweet spot such as this one, plants will endure cold nights in the 20s as if temperatures were above freezing.

The same patio on 95°F days in midsummer can be 10 degrees hotter or more than the air temperature in the yard. If the patio is surrounded by grass and shaded by trees, it will be cooler than the yard temperature. Under the dense canopy of an oak in the backyard, for example, the air will be at least 10 degrees cooler.

Microclimates exist in your yard, too. Find them by taking thermometer readings throughout your container gardening area, and watch for prevailing wind patterns as well. When you get to know your microclimates, you can use them to get a jump on the growing season in early spring, cool down overheated containers gardens in hot weather and shelter plants from sudden fall frosts.

FROSTS AND FREEZES

Weather is a factor even the most experienced gardener can't control. Unexpected freezes or frosts occur in every climate. Don't automatically accept the fact that all your plants are damaged or dead just because frost occurred while you slept. There is a big difference between a frost, freeze and killing freeze. To make things more confusing, different words are used to describe these cool-weather events in different parts of the country. Let's try to sort them out.

A light frost describes the formation of a thin layer of ice crystals on the ground and other surfaces. During the night, water in the warm air near the ground condenses and freezes on cool surfaces such as plants and lawns. The air temperature can be a degree or two above freezing (32°F) and a light frost

When dormant, hardy deciduous shrubs usually require a period of exposure to chilly temperatures.

Clear plastic helps capture the warmth of the sun while buffering plants from cold winds.

can occur. Some plants, such as tomatoes and impatiens, blacken and wither at the barest touch of frost. With others, the fine coating of ice is meaningless or even beneficial. Spinach, pansies and other plants planted in the fall flourish when lightly dusted with frost.

A freeze, on the other hand, which is often called hard frost in the Northeast and a hard freeze in the South, will kill tender plants and new leaf buds. When air temperatures are below 28°F for several hours or more, plant cells start to freeze all the way through. When they thaw, they rupture and the leaves wither. Hardy plants such as pansies, spinach and liriope may show little damage from a freeze if they have been able to gradually become accustomed to cold temperatures. However, a hard freeze signals the end of the season for summer annuals and the top parts of most perennials. Hardy shrubs and trees simply become dormant when freezes become frequent.

What all this means for container gardeners is to get ready to move plants you want to save from freezing weather before they become damaged. You can also cover plants with an old blanket to help get them through short periods of cold weather.

DEALING WITH HEAT, HUMIDITY AND RAINFALL

Heat is another factor gardeners cannot control, but there are ways to lessen its impact on your container plants. Container color is important in hot climates and those with warm summers, for white, light gray and beige reflect sunlight rather than absorb it. Dark containers such as black pots absorb the sun and heat up the soil. If the soil gets hot enough, plants die. Besides using light colored containers, you can keep plant roots cool in warm climates by mulching over the surfaces where plants are placed with a couple of inches of pine bark, pebbles, straw or even newspaper. Organic mulches such as bark slowly decompose and need occasional replenishing to maintain a two inch deep layer.

In all climates, watch where you place containers in hot weather. Stone, cement or brick surfaces reflect heat into containers when the sun beats down directly. If possible, move containers to a grassy area with less reflected ground heat or

Large containers hold more moisture than small ones—a requirement for big tropicals such as Australian tree fern.

brief downpours and the pebbles scattered about. Take steps to protect susceptible plants by positioning them out of the rain, under wide eaves or on covered porches. Put up gutters at eave edges to direct rain away and protect hanging plants.

CHANGING LIGHT

Except for those specially adapted to shade, most plants grow best where they receive at least eight hours of sunlight each day. In southern climates, six hours daily will do. You can move pots and tubs around to catch enough sunlight even if your yard or patio is shady part of the day. If plants receive too much shade, they grow tall and leggy, reaching for the sun.

Sunlight varies in intensity by the season. Eight hours of direct sun in July is not the same as eight hours in January or even May. Summer sun is intense and hot, because the sun is at its closest point to the earth then. Winter sun is the weakest, when the sun is farthest away. So a plant will require more hours of sunlight in winter, spring and fall than it will in summer. This is why many plants like a little afternoon shade in midsummer and crave full sun the rest of the year.

Plants can get a sunburn just like people do. Look for brown, crisp patches on exposed leaves and curled leaf edges if you suspect plants are suffering from too much sun. Fruit and vegetables can also be sunburned. There will be telltale brown patches on them, too. When these symptoms appear on tomato or pepper fruits, it is often called sunscald.

Plants raised indoors need about 14 hours of sunlight from south or west facing windows. That may be impossible to achieve without augmenting the natural window light with artificial light from a fluorescent fixture. An inexpensive 4-foot-long shop light hung a foot above plants will do the job. You may also want to paint the interior window area white or cover it with white material, for white reflects light back to the plants. Special horticultural fluorescent bulbs, positioned six inches above

into a shady portion of the patio or porch where surfaces are cooler.

If you have no sheltered place to move overheated containers, use shade cloth to cool them down. This translucent black or green fabric can be draped over plants or spread over a frame to shelter them. Shade cloth does not block out all the sunlight, but it reduces the intensity. Different grades are available that block from 15 percent to 75 percent of the sunlight. Look for shade cloth at garden centers and in mail order catalogs.

In many parts of the country, summer means high heat and humidity. Along with that sticky feeling comes an invitation to fungal diseases that thrive on damp plant leaves. To prevent leaf spots and mildews, space containers far apart so that air can circulate freely around foliage. Also water early in the day so that wet leaves and stems can dry in the sun. After a rain, shake off as much water from plant leaves as possible, especially if the rain comes towards nightfall.

Some plants such as fuschias and lamb's-ear suffer damage from rain, too. It flattens them and destroys their leaves. Hanging baskets full of impatiens or grape ivy hung under house eaves can be mangled in minutes from rain runoff that rolls off the roof and cascades into the baskets. Small pots of succulents anchored in gravel can be uprooted in plants, can supply all the light if a window is not available.

SHAPING AND THINNING

Many annual flowers and herbs have upright growth habits and don't bush out or spread naturally. When plants are young, frequent pinching of growth tips will force them to branch and grow wide. More better quality flowers are produced on bushy plants.

Pinching is an easy, fast way to prune tender growth. Take the top half inch of fleshy, new growth on a stem or runner between your thumb and index finger and press or pinch. The stem should snap off effortlessly. Repeat this pinching process on all stems that are six inches or so in length to create compact plants. You may want to pinch a plant several times, at three or four week intervals, for maximum stems and flowers.

Tip pruning of woody plants such as boxwood and rosemary is done in the same manner. New growth tips are often soft enough to pinch by hand, but use pruning shears if you find yourself having to twist and pull to shape your plants. Pruning fruit trees is much more complicated and is done in late winter, just before they produce new leaves. The first step in pruning fruit trees is to remove damaged or diseased wood. After that, the goal is to remove branches that are close together or very long, in order to give the plant an open, balanced shape. You can get detailed information on fruit tree pruning free from local agriculture extension agents, garden centers and at the library.

Thinning is another important favor you may need to do for your plants, especially if you start them from seeds. The simple rule of thumb to follow is to thin plants so that the leaves of adjoining plants barely touch. This is a crucial step in growing many vegetables from seed, and can help you grow much stockier annual flowers, as well. At the same time, container gardeners always crowd plants together in order to get the best show. As long as you provide plenty of water and fertilizer, plants can grow

Removing faded flowers encourages bushy growth and the formation of new blossoms.

very well in close spacing. If they shade each other too severely, try rotating the container one-quarter turn around each day so that each side of the container gets a chance at strong light.

CLEANING UP FOR WINTER

Annual flowers, many herbs and most vegetables are in decline by the time the first freeze approaches. Hardy perennials and shrubs vary in their response to winter. If special measures are needed, they are described in the plant profiles in the following chapters.

When the season for summer plants ends, empty and clean containers before storing them. Dump pot contents, soil included, in your compost bin or add to

Pinching back stem tips results in many more flowering branches on chrysanthemums.

flower beds but not if the plants were diseased. Scrub pots, tubs and window boxes with a stiff brush dipped in a light bleach solution (one tablespoon household bleach to a quart of warm water) to remove dirt, moss and other debris. Rinse and dry in the sun. Then store in a basement or garage that will remain above freezing. Even when empty, clay vessels and many ceramic ones will crack in freezing temperatures.

All soil blends, amendments such as peat moss and vermiculite and fertilizers should be sealed for winter storage. Close bags and boxes with tape or clothespins, and place them in containers such as large plastic boxes and trash cans with lids that lock on tightly. Soils and fertilizers will be good for another season if they are stored dry. Soils can be stored outdoors in freezing weather if they are sealed in moisture-proof containers. Fertilizers should be placed in a dry area that remains above freezing.

Prepare your leftover seeds for winter, too. Tape packets closed and place them in a zipper-type plastic bag. Push as much of the air out of the bag as you can before sealing it. Place the bag in the refrigerator until the next planting season. You might want to jot down some notes about which seeds did best in your container garden, when they bloomed or fruited and any problems or special pleasures you observed. Include these notes in the plastic bag with the seeds.

❦

Chapter 4

CONTAINER GARDENING STEP BY STEP

Whether you're planting a pot of parsley or creating an elaborate mixture of flowers and herbs, there are but 10 simple steps from start to finish. In this chapter, you will see exactly what to do, and perhaps pick up some useful pointers on color, style and seasonal appeal by studying six easy container compositions.

The examples shown here utilize new clay pots and packaged potting soil. When planting containers that have been used before, take a few minutes to clean them well before replanting them. Refer to Chapter 3, The Basics of Container Gardening, for a refresher course on potting soils and other practical matters. Some plants grow better if you doctor packaged potting soil by mixing in sand, peat moss, lime, sulfur or good soil dug from the ground. Look in the plant profiles in the chapters that follow for suggestions on selecting and growing these plants.

Putting together colorful container compositions is creative fun. Here the dwarf dahlias get their turn in the sun.

Container Gardening Step by Step

Step 1

In a roomy space that can be easily swept or rinsed clean, assemble your container, potting soil, hose or watering can and plants. Have gloves ready if you want to use them.

Step 2

Cover any large, open drainage holes in the container with a loose pile of broken pottery or large pebbles. Beneath these "rocks," you may place a single sheet of thin paper or newspaper or a small piece of polyester window screen material. The goal when covering the hole is to stop soil from leaking out while allowing for the easy drainage of extra water. The paper or screen material will also help keep small insects and crustaceans from entering through the hole.

Step 3

If you are using an unglazed clay container like the one here, dampen it well. Some gardeners like to soak small clay pots in water overnight to help them absorb water. This step is not necessary when planting in non-porous containers such as those made from plastic or fiberglass.

Step 4

Fill the container one-third full with potting soil. If you wish to add lime, fertilizer or other soil amendments to the mixture, sprinkle them atop the dry soil and mix in well with your hand, a small trowel or a large kitchen spoon. When planting tall, upright containers that are easily toppled, you may also add small stones or chunky gravel to the bottom layer of soil to give the container extra bottom weight.

Step 5

Thoroughly dampen the soil in the container, allow the water to drain through, and then dampen again. If you leave a dry

pocket in the bottom of a large container, it can be very difficult to properly saturate the pot later on.

Step 6

Add additional soil to within about six inches of the rim of the pot, or two inches from the rim of shallow window boxes or troughs. Again mix in soil amendments if desired.

Step 7

Soak again with water. This will cause the soil level to drop slightly. If you will be planting the container with small bed-

top. Gently remove the plant from its nursery pot, pulling the main stem as little as possible. Use your fingers to untangle any roots that have grown into a spiral around the bottom of the pot. Spread these roots out as you set the plant in the new container. In this example, the largest plant is 'Iceberg' rose. After the rose is situated, two more inches of soil are added and dampened to bring the soil level up to four inches from the rim—the right depth for planting the smaller companion plants that were purchased in four-inch pots.

Step 9

Position the smaller companion plants. In this composition, white 'Sonata' cosmos will help create a soft frame for the rose, and dainty 'Palace White lobelia' will gradually foam over the

ding plants that do not require deep planting, repeat the last two steps to bring the soil level to within two inches of the rim.

Step 8

With your largest plant still in its nursery pot, position it in the center of the container, or slightly to the rear of the center if you will be planting several smaller plants in the foreground. Dig a shallow depression in the soil if needed to adjust the depth so the plant will be only slightly deeper than it was in its nursery pot when the container is filled to within one inch of the

front edge. The cosmos are planted on either side of and behind the rose, with the lobelias placed close to the rim in the front of the planter. When handling these or any other potted bedding plants, untangle the bottom half-inch of roots as you plant. Fill the container nearly to the top with soil, and water well. When you are finished, the soil should completely cover the roots of the plants. After settling, it should be about one inch below the rim of the pot.

Step 10

Move the planted pot to its permanent home. For heavy pots, use a flat dolly on rollers or a wagon. To facilitate drainage, place small flat stones or purchased support feet beneath the container to raise it at least a half inch from the ground.

A simple arrangement of annuals can be composed quickly and enjoyed all summer. ❧

Profiles

Profile One
Bright Whites

PLANT LIST
1 floribunda rose 'Iceberg'
3 cosmos 'Sonata White'
4 lobelia 'Palace White'

SEASON The lobelia begins blooming as soon as it is planted, and the cosmos follow in time to spotlight the rose. With good care and hospitable weather, flowering will continue through most of the summer.

EXPOSURE Full sun is needed, but limited afternoon shade is beneficial where summers are hot. Display this composition where it can be enjoyed at night.

CONTAINER Any dark-colored container at least 14 inches wide will help anchor this all-white composition. Excellent drainage is crucial.

SOIL Use any high-quality potting soil for these plants. Roses strongly prefer a near-neutral pH. Check the pH in midsummer and scratch a light dusting of lime into the soil surface if needed.

WATER AND FERTILIZER Water as often as needed to support steady growth. Fertilize every two weeks during the summer.

OTHER MAINTENANCE Deadhead the rose and the cosmos promptly to encourage the production of new buds.

TIPS Dispose of lobelia and cosmos just before frost strikes. Fill any holes left behind with fresh potting soil, and mulch the base of the rose with peat moss, sand or sawdust. Allow the rose to become dormant, prune back lightly and hold it in a cool place through winter. In most climates, this rose can be kept outdoors through winter, wrapped lightly with burlap.

Profile Two
Herbal Rainbow

PLANT LIST
3 *Salvia elegans* 'American'
2 basil 'Dark Opal'
2 nasturtium 'Alaska'
2 parsley, curly type

SEASON Parsley and nasturtium like cool weather, so they will grow fast following spring planting. As the weather warms, salvia and basil will grow rapidly, and provide some shade for the smaller plants.

EXPOSURE At least a half day of sun is needed in most climates. In hot summer areas, filtered shade or full afternoon shade will help the salvia and basil stay lush and full.

CONTAINER Good alternate choices include a squat, chimney shaped clay pot, a square Chippendale-type planter (available in wood or plastic) or a 14-inch plastic planter.

SOIL These plants are not particularly demanding, but good drainage is essential.

WATER AND FERTILIZER The inside of this container will quickly be filled by roots, so you may need to drench the pot two or three times (a few minutes apart) to thoroughly moisten the soil inside. Drench thoroughly when the basil or salvia begin to droop. Add fertilizer to the water every third time you water.

OTHER MAINTENANCE As soon as the basil and salvia begin to grow, pinch off their main growing points to encourage the plants to develop more bushy stems. Clip off old salvia blossoms promptly. Harvest basil flowers often for garnishes.

TIPS Since you may eat parsley and the leaves or flowers of both nasturtium and basil, grow this masterpiece away from plants that receive pesticide sprays. Don't eat the salvia, though.

Profile Three
A Potted Forest

PLANT LIST
1 *Abutilon hybridum* 'Luteus'
3 *Lamium maculatum* 'Pink Pewter'
3 impatiens 'Accent Coral'

SEASON If brought indoors in winter, the abutilon and the impatiens will grow as ever-greens. Annual impatiens brings extra color during the warm summer months.

EXPOSURE A half day of sun will keep the abutilon happy. Its arching branches filter sunlight that reaches the smaller plants, which require more shade. Should the abutilon fail to bloom, give it more sun.

CONTAINER This composition requires a roomy pot of at least 14 inches that drains well. Good options include a wood box, a squat chimney-shaped pot or an Oriental-style glazed container.

SOIL All of these plants like moist soil. Add peat moss to the potting mixture, along with a little garden soil to give the container plenty of weight.

WATER AND FERTILIZER Provide water before the soil dries out (the impatiens will droop readily when dry). During the summer, fertilize every two weeks. In winter, limit fertilizer to light monthly feedings.

OTHER MAINTENANCE The abutilon needs regular pinching to help sculpt the almost vine-like branches into a pleasing shape. Watch for whiteflies and scale in summer, and treat promptly with insecticidal soap or light horticultural oil.

TIPS Rejuvenate lamium yearly by shearing it back to the soil in late winter. It is an aggressive spreader. Dig out extra plants when they become too thick.

Profile Four
Early Summer Blueprint

PLANT LIST
3 coreopsis 'Sunray'
3 *Salvia farinacea* 'Victoria Blue'
3 petunia 'Ultra Sky Blue'
2 sweet alyssum 'Snow Crystals'

SEASON Following spring planting, this container bouquet reaches its peak of color in early summer. Regular removal of dead blooms (deadheading) will keep the plants in bloom most of the summer. The coreopsis can be held over winter in a protected place outdoors.

EXPOSURE Full sun is needed to keep these flowers growing strong. In hot summer areas, a few hours of shade is acceptable.

CONTAINER Any container with good drainage is fine. A 14-inch plastic pot will ease watering chores in hot summer climates.

SOIL Any potting soil will please these easy-to-grow plants. Place a handful of slow-release pelleted fertilizer in the bottom third of the container when planting.

WATER AND FERTILIZER Provide water as needed to keep the soil lightly moist. If the petunias wilt, step up your watering schedule. Mix fertilizer into the water every two weeks.

OTHER MAINTENANCE Clip off faded flowers promptly. Even with deadheading, the coreopsis will likely stop blooming by late summer. Shear back petunias and sweet alyssum if the stems become long and leggy.

TIPS In most climates, you can dig, divide and repot the coreopsis in fall, and add new annuals to the pot the following spring. The salvia is not as winter hardy, and is not likely to survive winter outdoors north of Zone 7.

Profile Five
Tropical Trio

PLANT LIST
1 *Fuchsia triphylla* 'Gartenmeister Bonstedt'
1 tuberous begonia 'Nonstop'
4 impatiens 'Accent White'

SEASON Following spring planting, these tropical flowers will begin blooming after the weather warms in early summer, and continue to bloom until fall. None of them can tolerate frost or cold weather.

EXPOSURE Good light is needed, but not all day direct sun. The fuchsia and begonia are easily damaged by heavy rainfall, and will keep their looks best if grown on a protected patio or terrace.

CONTAINER Any container at least 14 inches in diameter is good for this composition. The orange-red exterior of the fuchsia blossoms works well with the color of terra-cotta.

SOIL Use a sterile potting soil amended with sand and peat moss. These plants need constantly moist soil and excellent drainage.

WATER AND FERTILIZER Water often to keep the soil constantly moist. In summer, mix fertilizer into the water every 10 days, or more often if the plants grow slowly.

OTHER MAINTENANCE You may need to clip back impatiens stems to make room for the begonia, which will bloom best from midsummer to fall. Groom fuchsia by trimming off leggy stems after the flowers fade.

TIPS When frosty weather is imminent, pull out the impatiens, and then gently dig the begonia and set it in a dry pot to cure for a day or so. Prune back fuchsia by half, and keep it indoors through winter as a blooming houseplant.

Profile Six
Salvia Showcase

PLANT LIST
1 Mexican bush sage *Salvia leucantha*
1 zonal geranium 'Bubble Gum'
2 narrowleaf zinnias *Z. angustifolia* 'Classic White'
2 sweet alyssum 'Easter Bonnet Deep Rose'

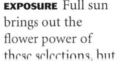

SEASON From spring planting, this bouquet changes its look as summer unfolds. Early on, the alyssum provides color, followed by the geranium and zinnias. From midsummer to frost, the salvia produces dozens of graceful purple flower spikes.

EXPOSURE Full sun brings out the flower power of these selections, but partial afternoon shade will give them a welcome break in very hot summer climates.

CONTAINER The orange tones of terra-cotta work well with the purple sage, but a gray clay or plastic pot, or even weathered concrete, would create a cooler, more subdued color combination.

SOIL These plants will adapt to any potting soil, but they do need excellent drainage. Place a one-inch layer of rocks or stones in the bottom of the container before filling it.

WATER AND FERTILIZER Provide water lightly and often, for these are drought tolerant plants that resent very wet roots. Fertilize every two weeks throughout the summer.

OTHER MAINTENANCE Deadhead often to keep the planting looking neat. After the sage comes into bloom, lop off entire branches near the plant's base when the flowers fade.

TIPS Following frost, dispose of the annuals and cut the sage back close to the soil line. Hold the sage in a cool garage or basement through winter. The next spring, divide the plant into two or three new ones by cutting through the root clump with a sharp knife.

Chapter 5

❋

QUICK COLOR FROM ANNUALS

*M*ost of the plants that you find displayed in plastic cellpacks at garden centers are annuals. Technically speaking, annual plants are those that complete their life cycle within the span of one growing season; they sprout from seeds, flower, produce the next generation of seeds and then die. A few of the plants we know as annuals can survive winter and return for a second season if conditions are just right, such as dusty miller, pansies and snapdragons. However, their flower power is usually so weak in the second year that pampering them through a second season is hardly worth the trouble. Instead, plan on filling containers with healthy young plants every year.

Annual flowers are popular among container gardeners for good reason. Compared to all other types of plants—perennials, bulbs, even shrubs—well-situated annuals produce many more

Crowding pansies and petunias into a window box leads to non-stop blooms to enjoy from both sides of the window.

Begonias team up with Japanese maple to dress a formal entryway.

impatiens, coleus and zinnia, grow best after the weather has warmed in late spring or early summer. Those regarded as cool-season annuals give their best show when grown where nights remain cool all summer, or when used to color up the spring season in warmer climates. A few annuals are truly winter hardy, and can be planted in fall in many areas. When given the luxury of spending their winters developing large, dependable root systems, these hardy annual flowers provide a strong splash of color in spring, before more warm-natured summer annuals are ready to bloom. See the box *Annuals for All Seasons* to find the weather preferences of the most popular annuals for containers.

GETTING STARTED WITH ANNUALS

You can grow your own annual plants from seed, and a few are so easy to grow this way that they are seldom sold in six packs. The simplest method for starting seeds is to save some plastic cellpacks from purchased bedding plants, clean them well with warm soapy water and then fill them to the top with a sterile soilless mix. Thoroughly moisten the filled containers, and then plant two to three seeds in each compartment, usually about a quarter inch deep. Enclose the planted cellpack in a clear plastic bag (to help retain moisture), and place it in good light (but not direct sun) for three to six days, or until you see sprouts breaking through the surface. Then remove the bags and place the little plants in a sunny spot where you can easily water them every day if needed to keep the planting medium constantly moist. The box at right indicates the annual flowers that are the best candidates for beginning seed starters.

Most other annual flowers take so long to grow to transplanting size that buying them as bedding plants is a good investment. For example, begonia seeds are the size of dust particles, and they take up to 12 weeks to grow to transplanting size. So a dollar spent on a six pack of plants is a dollar well spent.

blossoms and over a much longer period of time than more long-lived plants. In all climates, annuals are the main source of color in most container bouquets, window boxes and deck and patio gardens.

Annuals are also quite flexible when it comes to the company they keep. Most of the annuals that grow best in containers develop a tight network of thin, fibrous roots that coexist easily with the thick, heavy roots of perennials and

flowers that grow from fleshy tubers or bulbs. When you need small companion plants to dress the edges of containers planted with larger, hardier plants, annuals such as sweet alyssum, lobelia or schizanthus may be the perfect choice.

You will get the best performance from annual flowers by growing them in the type of weather they like best. Annual flowers whose ancestors came from tropical parts of the world, such as

Annuals for All Seasons

YOUR LOCAL GARDEN CENTER WILL TAKE some of the guesswork out of knowing when to plant annual flowers, for the plants are usually sold at the best time for planting. Use the lists below as a shopping guide to help you select good annuals for each part of the growing season.

HARDY ANNUALS

Plant these in fall in Zones 7 to 10, or very early in spring in northern areas.
Sweet alyssum, dianthus, forget-me-not, pansy, snapdragon

COOL-SEASON ANNUALS

Buy plants or start seeds from late winter to early spring so they can enjoy every minute of weather that is cool but not freezing.
Brachycome, calendula, candytuft, cosmos, lobelia, nasturtium, nierembergia, stock, sweet pea

WARM-SEASON ANNUALS

These plants grow best after nights warm to above 50°F. Use them for color during the warmest part of summer.
Black-eyed Susan vine, celosia, coleus, impatiens, lantana, melampodium, salvia, vinca, zinnia

ADAPTABLE ANNUALS

These flowers can adapt to big weather changes, including cool and hot spells. Use them as mainstays in your container plantings.
Begonia, dusty miller, marigold, nicotiana, petunia, salvia, torenia, verbena

---

Buying your annuals as bedding plants has other advantages, too. Many of the newer varieties have been specially bred to produce one or two blossoms very early, at exactly the time they hit garden center shelves. When you can see the exact color of the flowers, you can get a much better idea of how you might use them in your containers. If you plan to mix a number of different annuals in container bouquets, you can get a preview of your final composition by simply arranging different cellpacks side by side to see how the flowers and foliage look together.

Early shoppers will find the best selection of plants, but you can also expect the selection to change as spring gets under way. For example, pansies and snapdragons are sold quite early in the spring (and in fall in many areas), whereas you may need to wait until April to buy impatiens, which struggle to grow in cool weather. Buy your annuals from a retailer who keeps them nicely watered, and gives them the amount of light they need to stay in good condition. The plants you find at discount stores are just as good as those from upscale nurseries, provided the plants have received proper care.

> **Annual Flowers that are the Best Candidates for Beginning Seed Starters**
>
> baby's breath
> bidens
> black-eyed Susan vine
> cosmos
> marigold
> melampodium
> morning glory
> nasturtium
> scarlet runner bean
> sunflower
> sweet pea
> zinnia

ADOPTING ANNUAL FLOWERS

As soon as you get your bedding plants home, water them well and snip off any broken stems. Also look at the bottom of the cellpacks to see if the roots are so extensive that they are reaching out of the drainage holes. Petunias, pansies and many other annual flowers have very crowded roots by the time they reach stores. To keep from delaying their progress, work with your most root-bound plants first.

Regardless of what you see when you look at the bottoms of your containers, keep your plants in a semi-shady place if you must wait several days or longer before planting them. At least an hour before actually shifting your annuals from the seedling containers to larger pots, boxes or baskets, drench them thoroughly with a weak solution of water soluble fertilizer. Wet roots slide out of tight quarters much more easily than dry ones.

PLANTING ANNUALS IN CONTAINERS

Some annuals are susceptible to diseases that can be carried over from one year to the next in potting soil, so it is best to start with clean containers and fresh potting mixtures. If you must clean a number of containers, fill a large tub or plastic wheelbarrow with warm, soapy water, and let the containers soak until they can be easily cleaned with a stiff brush. Then rinse and you're ready to begin.

Place a few stones or bits of broken clay flowerpot in the bottom of each container if you think the plants will benefit from extra weight or improved drainage. Then fill the container to within four inches of the top with your selected potting medium. Remove bedding plants from their pots or cellpacks by pinching and pushing them from the bottom rather than trying to pull them out by their main stem. Hold the plant upside-down, with the stem and leaves between your fingers, and use your other hand to gently unwind or break apart roots that have formed a tight mass in

*F*REQUENTLY YOU WILL FIND YOURSELF with leftover bedding plants. You can easily hold on to these orphans by planting them in small individual containers and setting them aside in an out-of-the-way place. Save the four-inch plastic pots in which most perennials are sold for this job. After shifting annuals from two-inch cellpacks to four-inch pots, the plants will continue to develop. With many species, it helps to pinch off the highest growing tip so bushy side branches will begin to grow. Expect the repotted bedding plants to become rootbound again and to be ready for another move after about a month.

the bottom of the containers. Spread the roots out as you set the plants in their summer homes. When all the plants are where you want them, add additional potting soil almost to the top of the container. Water thoroughly, and add more potting soil if needed. If you like, you can cover the top of the soil with a thin layer of finely shredded bark

mulch or a few handfuls of dry sphagnum moss.

CARING FOR ANNUAL BOUQUETS

Many of the most popular annual flowers are often described as "self-cleaning." This means that as old blossoms fade, they quickly disappear with

no help from you. Begonias, impatiens, nierembergias and annual vincas are good examples of self-cleaning annuals. Maintenance for them consists of nothing more than routine watering and fertilizing.

Less tidy annuals will look better and flower longer if you pinch or snip off dead flowers every few days. This procedure, called deadheading, simply means removing dead flowers. Marigolds, pansies, petunias and many other annuals benefit greatly from regular deadheading. Avoid tugging or twisting stems when deadheading. If a good finger pinch does not cleanly sever the stem, use small scissors or pruning shears.

Another method of grooming annuals, called shearing back, involves trimming back large numbers of faded flowers and wasted stems at the same time. Whenever you notice that an an-

Cascades of purple lobelia and lavender alyssum tie together a colorful arrangement of annuals.

Three levels of color from strong-blooming marigolds, petunias and verbenas enrich an entryway

nual flower appears leggy and exhausted, but you can see new green leaf buds trying to grow from the centers of the plants, use pruning shears to cut back the plant by half its size. Follow up with water and fertilizer, and you may see a heavy flush of new flowers in about a month.

REPLACING TIRED BLOOMERS

No annuals flower forever, and only experience will tell you how long to expect specific annuals to provide good color in your container garden. When only one type of annual is growing in a container, and that annual fails, replacing it is a simple matter of dumping out the pot, cleaning it, and starting over with something new.

But what if you have planted a large container bouquet that includes a half dozen types of annuals, and one or two of the plants suddenly shrivels and dies? This often happens with cool-season annuals, such as sweet alyssum and lobelia, which fortunately are often planted near the edges of containers. Take a small knife, cut out the two or three inch square of soil directly under the withered plant, and pull it out like a plug. Then, either fill in the hole with fresh potting soil or fill in with a replacement plant appropriate for the season. Ageratum, melampodium, pentas and narrowleaf zinnias make good summer replacements for weary flowers that give out in summer.

A Gallery of Annual Flowers

Almost any annual will grow in a container, but the following list of 50 includes the most popular and rewarding annuals to work with in pots, baskets and windowboxes. Since annuals are so easy to use in mixed bouquets, good companions are noted within each plant profile. Of course, your choices of plant partners need not be limited to these. With annuals, there is virtually no end to the unique living pictures you can create by experimenting with different colors, flower forms and foliage.

Ageratum
Ageratum houstonianum

The unusual blue flowers of ageratum appear as softly textured puffs, perfect for mixing with coarser flowers or shrubs. Ageratum also comes in white, but as the white flowers wither they appear dirty and unkempt. Blue cultivars sold as bedding plants are usually 6-inch dwarfs that spread into small mounds. Comparatively rare 2-foot varieties must be started from seeds. Ageratum loves sun, hot weather and regular water, and can adapt to most types of potting soil. Deadhead to keep plants looking neat, and fertilize at least monthly. Late in the summer, look for low stems attempting to establish new roots. These may be snipped off and transplanted to new compositions to enjoy in the fall.

HOW TO USE
To make the most of its unusual texture, let ageratum accompany red salvias, orange marigolds or zinnias. Shallow-rooted ageratum is also a good summer cover for pots in which spring-flowering bulbs are resting beneath the surface.

Alyssum, sweet
Lobularia maritima

Sweet alyssum is the most useful of small annuals for mixed container

Frothy sweet alyssum.

bouquets. The dainty 4-inch plants spread into a mossy mass covered with tiny, lightly scented white, pink or purple flowers. Sweet alyssum prefers cool weather and at least a half day of sun. Seedlings are widely available as bedding plants, or you can start seeds in flats in late winter. When the plants are more than one inch tall, cut out 2-inch-square chunks and transplant them to container bouquets. Plants may struggle to bloom in the heat of late summer, and then give up completely. Sweet alyssum is often winter hardy in Zones 8 and 9.

HOW TO USE
Plant sweet alyssum beneath taller annuals, trees or open shrubs, slip plants into herbal bouquets and use liberally as filler plants in window boxes or complicated mixtures. Place sweet alyssum near the edges of containers so it can gently spill over the sides.

Aster
Aster hybrids

The asters sold in containers for fall display are perennials, but most people grow them as annuals. Like chrysanthemums, these plants develop buds and blooms when the days become short in late summer. When in bloom, they are covered with dainty blue or pink blossoms. Purchase plants when they become available in midsummer, and transplant them to your containers of

choice. Add a half-dose of fertilizer to the water you give them, and keep the containers in a sunny spot. Blooms usually hold until after the first frost. True annual asters are subject to several diseases, but are worth trying from seed started in spring.

HOW TO USE
Display containers of pastel asters near yellow chrysanthemums, yellow marigolds or other plants that reflect the hues of autumn.

Baby's breath
Gypsophilia elegans

The stiff baby's breath florists use is a perennial plant, but the annual form works best in containers. Available in white or lavender, this fast little annual often tops out at 12 inches tall. Baby's breath grows in sun or partial shade, and adapts to any type of potting soil. Bedding plants are somewhat uncommon, but seeds are easy to sprout and grow. Sow new seeds every few weeks to maintain a good supply of seedlings. Even when perfectly happy, annual baby's breath may stay in flower for only a few weeks.

HOW TO USE
White annual baby's breath is a fantastic filler for container bouquets where you are mixing several colors and textures. Crowding often causes the flowering stems to become lax, which enhances their appeal.

Begonia
Begonia semperflorens

Extremely uniform and always well groomed, the familiar bedding begonias, also called fibrous-rooted begonias, are the plants of choice for filling identical pots in formal arrangements. Red leaf color is often paired with red flowers; the reds contrast beautifully with white or pink flowered selections with predominantly green

Stalwart begonias.

leaves. These begonias will grow in sun or shade, in any potting medium and thrive with regular water and monthly fertilization. They require no other maintenance, and stay in bloom continuously from planting until frost. In fall, you can bring your best begonia containers indoors for a few more weeks of color.

HOW TO USE

Flank your front door with large matching pots of begonias, or plant them in several smaller containers to bring continuity to your collection of containerized plants. In bouquet plantings, begonias mix well with sweet alyssum, nierembergia or English ivy.

Bidens
Bidens ferulifolia

Bidens is not well known, for its free-wheeling habit is often unwelcome in manicured beds. It's a different story in containers, where bidens' 20-inch nimble stems easily stretch through the foliage of companion plants. Best in good sunlight, bidens produces sunny yellow flowers for several weeks. If purchased plants are not available, start seeds in flats or pots in spring, and transplant to roomier containers

when they are 4 inches tall. Any potting medium is fine. Trim off stems after flowers shrivel.

HOW TO USE

Bidens works wonders in whimsical compositions in unusual containers, or it can be counted upon for yellow highlights in mixed bouquet plantings. The slender stems will form a halo around bold nasturtiums or geraniums, and or you can use them to soften the edges of any large composition.

Black-eyed Susan vine
Thunbergia alata

Exuberant in sun or afternoon shade, black-eyed Susan vine's yellow-orange flowers are actually tubular, and it's their dark, hollow throats that make them appear to have black eyes. White-flowered varieties flower with less enthusiasm, but any thunbergia will produce a lush cover of green foliage. Use a soil-based potting medium, and start seeds in late winter. They are very easy to sprout and grow, and plants often reseed. This vine needs no help scrambling up a fence or trellis, or you can allow it to spill out of a container and onto the ground below.

HOW TO USE

Black-eyed Susan vine will quickly overtake any other plants you place nearby. It looks lovely wandering about the base of statuary, and makes a quick and easy cover for a chain link fence.

Brachycome
Brachycome iberidifolia

Commonly known as Swan River daisy, brachycome's slender stems fall over naturally until the plants become soft green puffs studded with small mauve flowers. The ferny foliage also offers useful texture when the plants reach their mature size of 12 inches. Bedding plants are often available, or you can start seeds indoors in late winter. Any potting soil will do, but make sure the plants get a half day of sun, plenty of fresh air and fertilizer every two weeks. Shear back after the first flowers shrivel to bring about a second flush of color.

HOW TO USE

Brachycome's soft texture and cool color can fill a container with ease, but you will need at least four plants to fill a 6-inch pot. Also use brachycome to lend a gentle touch of pink to the edge of a complex container composition. It is outstanding with soft yellow or white flowers, and dazzles when used in combination with gray and chartreuse foliage plants.

Brachycome.

Browallia
Browallia speciosa

A glorious basket plant for spots that receive only a few hours of sun, browallia often stays in bloom continuously from spring until frost. In spring, plants are widely available in small containers or already situated in hanging baskets. Although white browallias are available, the strongest color is this plant's ancestral blue hue. Mature stem length is 10 to 14 inches. Use a planting medium that holds moisture well, and do not allow baskets to dry out completely. If they do, soak in a tub of water for an hour

A basket of blue browallia.

to rehydrate the soil. Fertilize browallia every two weeks during warm summer weather.

HOW TO USE
A basket of brilliant blue browallia will get plenty of attention with no assistance. For a change of pace, mix browallia with frilly white cascading petunias. In upright pots, browallia pairs well with white sweet alyssum, nierembergia or dwarf white petunias.

Calendula
Calendula officinalis

Also known as pot marigolds, calendulas boast traditional marigold colors, but the blossoms are flat, like daisies, and more refined. They also require cool weather, and can survive light

Yellow calendulas.

frosts. Height ranges from 8-inch dwarfs to more stately 30-inch plants. Sow seeds outdoors in early spring, or buy bedding plants. Calendulas need sun and regular water, but they are not picky about soil. Fertilize every two to three weeks, and remove spent flowers to prolong the bloom time. In warm climates, replace calendulas with more heat tolerant flowers in midsummer.

HOW TO USE
Calendulas can do a fine job of filling containers by themselves, or you can create powerful color contrast with purple pansies. Accompany calendulas with the white of perennial candytuft if you prefer a cleaner, lighter look. When mixing calendulas with several other flowers, use a soft gray foliage plant such as lamb's-ear to help tie different bright colors together.

Candytuft
Iberis umbellata

Annual candytuft comes in an array of pink hues as well as white. In mid- to late spring, the 10-inch-tall plants become covered with rounded blossom clusters, which are sometimes fragrant. From Zone 7 southward, start seeds in fall and overwinter flats or

planted containers outdoors in a cold frame, for they are quite hardy. Use a heavy potting mixture for fall planting. In other areas get bedding plants established in containers as early as possible. Light fertilization and trimming promote repeat blooming, but heat cuts the flowering season short.

HOW TO USE
Combine annual candytuft with pansies, dianthus and snapdragons, which also can be started in fall in many areas. This candytuft also makes a good companion for late tulips or container-grown deciduous trees.

Celosia
Celosia argentea plumosa

Hot summer sun brings out the best in plume-type celosias, which come in red, yellow, apricot and pink. Some red varieties have distinctive reddish foliage. Height ranges from 8 to 24 inches. Purchase bedding plants in spring, or start seeds outdoors after the last frost. Pinch off the first plume that forms to induce branching. Use any potting mixture for celosias, and fertilize every two weeks. Cut off old plumes to promote the growth of fresh new ones. Cockscomb celosias also may be used in containers, though they are not as versatile as those that produce feathery plumes. All celosias

Dwarf pink plume celosias.

deteriorate by the time frost threatens in the fall.

HOW TO USE

Use plume celosias as central exclamation points in compositions made up of other heat-tolerant annuals such as gomphrena, sanvitalia and zinnia. Dusty miller helps tone down celosia's bright colors.

Coleus
Solenostemon scutellarioides

The richly colored leaves of coleus come in a nearly endless array of

Light and bright coleus.

striking colors and patterns, and the leaves themselves may be large and smooth or finely cut and almost ruffled. They thrive in light shade, and can adapt to any potting mixture if they are watered and fertilized regularly. Bedding plants are widely available. Pinch off flower spikes as they appear. If you want new plants to use in fall compositions, take 4-inch stem cuttings in mid-summer and set them to root in a sterile, soilless mix. They will strike new roots and be ready to transplant in only a month.

HOW TO USE

Coleus can be used in hanging baskets, window boxes or incorporated into bouquet plantings. Match foliage hues with the blossom colors of impatiens, petunias, salvias or tuberous begonias. Any flower that blooms in soft lavender shades is amplified when planted with yellow or chartreuse coleus.

Simple single cosmos blossoms.

Cosmos
Cosmos species

Dwarf forms of this cottage garden favorite produce ferny foliage and cheery flowers ideal for container bouquets. In cool climates, choose *Cosmos bipinnatus* 'Sonata', available in white, red or pink. In warmer areas, sulphur cosmos (*C. sulphureus*) is a fine source of bright yellow, orange and red. Height of these selections is less than 2 feet. Start with either seeds or bedding plants, and use any type of potting soil. Fertilize at least monthly, and pinch off dead flowers to keep plants looking neat.

HOW TO USE

The finely cut leaves of cosmos bring a light touch to complex compositions, and the slender flower stems often bend and twist to create interesting lines. These flowers work well with a broad palette of other annuals, including lobelia, petunia and verbena. Or try them with dahlias, alliums and other summer bulbs.

Dianthus
Dianthus hybrids

Many of the "annual" dianthus found among bedding plants will grow as perennials for a couple of years, but

Wine red dianthus.

they are best grown as fall to spring annuals in Zones 6 to 10, or as summer annuals farther north. Colors include many pinks (the strongest hues) as well as white, red and some bicolors. Give dianthus a gritty but rich potting mixture, plenty of sun, and fertilize monthly when the plants are actively growing. They typically become mounds of color for about six weeks in early summer and then bloom very little for the remainder of the season.

HOW TO USE

When planting in fall, stud containers with tidbits of hardy gray foliage plants such as artemisias or lamb's-ear. In spring, you can use dianthus as a blooming ground cover beneath upright flowers such as blue salvias or peacock orchids.

Dusty miller
Senecio cineraria

For container gardeners, dusty miller is in a class of its own. Its cool gray foliage spotlights other plants with luminous light, and it can adapt to any growing conditions except deep shade. Some cultivars have deeply serrated leaves, while others have a smoother texture. Height ranges from 8 to 12 inches, depending on variety. All are

Icy gray leaves of dusty miller.

Forget-me-not.

'Strawberry Fields' gomphrena.

widely available as spring bedding plants. Dusty miller often survives winter in mild winter areas, but 2-year-old plants look tattered compared to younger ones. Instead of keeping them for a second season, take tender young stem cuttings from over-wintered plants first thing in spring, and set them to root in a damp soilless mix. They will be ready to transplant to container bouquets in about a month.

HOW TO USE

Dusty miller goes with everything, and does different magic depending on how you use it. Pair it with hot red salvias or bright orange marigolds for startling contrast, or let dusty miller fuse soft pinks and blues when you want the mood to stay cool and relaxing.

Forget-me-not
Myosotis species

An old-fashioned favorite, little blue forget-me-nots make easy work of coloring up early spring in spots that receive only a few hours of sun. The 8- to 12-inch plants with dark green, woolly leaves grow into loose mounds, but they must be planted in fall. Start seeds in late summer so the seedlings will be big enough to transplant before hard freezes begin. Give forget-me-nots a soft, peaty

potting mixture, and keep planted containers outdoors in the cold through winter. Dispose of plants when they stop flowering in early summer.

HOW TO USE

In small containers, team up forget-me-nots with snow white perennial candytuft, which often blooms at the same time. In fall, when you fill containers with tulips or daffodils, stud the soil surface with a few forget-me-nots.

Geranium

See Geranium (on page 80), under perennials

Geraniums can be grown as annuals, or you can keep them indoors through winter.

Gomphrena
Gomphrena species

Like rounded gumdrops, the individual white, pink or strawberry orange blossoms of gomphrena persist for several weeks before shattering and making room for more. Purchase seedlings in late spring, and set them in containers after the weather has turned warm, for they crave heat. The upright plants eventually reach 20 inches, and flower best in strong sun. Snip off the oldest flowers to encourage the development of new branches. Gomphrena is sometimes sold as globe amaranth. The plants accept any potting mixture that drains well, and tolerate dry conditions better than most other summer flowers.

HOW TO USE

The shape of gomphrena's blossoms introduce a unique flower form to container bouquets. They partner well with any hot weather flower, such as lantana, marigold, vinca or zinnias, and provide welcome color highlights to containers planted primarily with foliage plants.

Heliotrope
Heliotropium arborescens

Heliotrope is actually a tropical perennial, but rooted cuttings are sold in spring alongside seedlings of other

Fragrant heliotrope.

Deep rose impatiens.

Lantana, trained to a standard form.

summer flowers. The flowers are broad umbels of tiny purple blossoms, which form atop dark green, heavily textured foliage. The feature that makes heliotrope so desirable is its vanilla-like fragrance, which can fill a patio or deck with its perfume. When planted in containers that receive partial shade, heliotrope grows to about 18 inches tall. Provide a rich potting medium, and water before the soil dries out completely. Fertilize every two weeks until blossoms form, then taper off as fall approaches.

HOW TO USE

A large container planted with three heliotrope plants is a masterpiece in itself. Try adding a pair of white petunias or a trailing collar of variegated English ivy or vinca major to create riveting contrast.

Impatiens
Impatiens hybrids

For bringing color to shady areas that get only a few hours of sun, impatiens are the annuals of choice. They are available in white, cool pastels or bright reds and salmon shades. There are also double forms. The most popular impatiens grow to less than one foot tall, and form mounds of color that never need grooming. A more sun-tolerant type of impatiens, called

New Guinea impatiens, are more upright and often have purplish foliage. Either type of impatiens will be happy when given a peaty soil mixture that retains water well, for their roots must be kept constantly moist. To reduce your watering chores, choose large plastic or fiberglass containers for impatiens. In warm summer weather when the plants are growing rapidly, add fertilizer to the water once a week.

HOW TO USE

Impatiens have an elegant form that can be combined with other shade plants, such as caladiums, but in windowboxes and large pots they look beautiful on their own. Place like colors together in individual containers, and arrange the pots in groups. If you have been frustrated when trying to keep impatiens watered after planting them in the ground, try planting them in plastic nursery liners, and place the planted pots among larger flowers growing in beds.

Lantana
Lantana camara

A great favorite of butterflies, lantana has long been regarded as a semi-tropical shrub. In Zones 9 and 10 it is a shrub indeed, but in other locations lantana is increasingly used as a summer bedding plant. Flowers may be yellow or multi-colored clusters of pink, purple, orange and yellow. Most selections have green leaves, but the yellow-flowered 'Samantha' cultivar has light green leaves edged with

cream. All lantanas like full sun or slight shade, and quickly branch to form a colorful mass of flowers and foliage up to two feet tall. Lantanas need warm growing conditions, but require only light fertilization. A rich but sandy soil is more to their liking than soilless mixes.

HOW TO USE

When the cool-weather annuals you started in early spring begin to wane, replace them with lantanas. Two or three plants will quickly fill a large 5-gallon container. Good companions include Russian sage and yellow cosmos.

Lobelia
Lobelia erinus

The lobelias most loved by container gardeners are small cascading plants that cover themselves with dainty blue, rose pink or white flowers in early summer. When lobelia is in bloom, the narrow green leaves are almost hidden

Lobelia.

by the flowers, which often have contrasting white throats. Less than 6 inches in height and twice as wide, lobelias foam over the edges of containers. Look for the 'Fountain' cultivar when buying bedding plants. Give lobelias at least five hours of good sun each day, use any soil mix that holds moisture well and fertilize plants every two weeks to promote strong growth. Where summers are warm, lobelias put on their best show in May and June. In cool climates, lobelias will flower all summer if sheared back once in July.

HOW TO USE

Line the edges of large pots and window boxes with this versatile plant. Pair pink petunias with blue or pink lobelias, or team up red geraniums with white selections. Lobelias are always welcome around the edges of complex container bouquets.

Marigold
Tagetes species

Marigolds are so easy to grow that they are naturals for low-maintenance containers. Give them full sun and a rather heavy soil mixture, and deadhead often to keep them neat and encourage new growth. Two-foot African marigolds can work as central subjects in container bouquets, or you can look for small-flowered marigolds with much finer textured foliage, such as the 14-inch signet or gem marigolds. In addition to using purchased seedlings in spring, start a second crop of seeds in early July. These late seedlings make perfect replacements for spent spring annuals, and are absolutely dazzling in the fall when trees begin to show their bright autumn colors.

HOW TO USE

Individual pots teeming with mounds of marigolds will brighten a sunny deck or patio by themselves. In the fall, keep small 6-inch pots of dwarf marigolds handy to flank larger pots of chrysanthemums.

Melampodium
Melampodium paludosum

Sometimes known as medallion flower, melampodium is a steady producer of starry yellow flowers. It is a champion at thriving under hot, humid conditions that aggravate other flowers. When grown in pots, melampodium usually stays under 14 inches tall. The plants form neat self-cleaning mounds. Grow them in full sun, in a soil-based mix, and water before the foliage shows signs of wilting (midday wilting is normal). Melampodium is often available in six packs in the spring, or you can start seeds in early summer and use the plants as replacements for cool-weather annuals.

HOW TO USE

Mounds of melampodium are ideal for hiding the skinny ankles of taller zinnias or even okra, or they can be given their own low containers. They can also be the upright feature in containers planted with vigorous annual vines such as morning glory or black-eyed Susan vine.

Morning glory
Ipomoea species

Morning glory vines can easily reach 8 feet in length, but a few varieties sold as dwarf morning glories trail only 1 to 2 feet. You can grow the larger ones, including the fragrant night blooming moon vine (*Ipomoea alba*) in large stationary containers, but you will need to train the vines up a sturdy string trellis or fence. Morning glory vines also can be pruned regularly to keep them from taking over too much space. Start seeds directly in the containers after the weather has warmed, in a heavy soil-based potting mixture, and fertilize monthly. Morning glories can handle either full sun or partial shade.

HOW TO USE

Because they are so vigorous, consider morning glories a singular type of container plant. Dwarf varieties make interesting plants for hanging baskets.

Nasturtium
Tropaeolum species

Nasturtiums bloom freely through spring and summer, usually in bright yellow, orange or red. The 'Alaska' cultivar has attractive variegated

Marigold.

Melampodium.

Nasturtiums.

foliage. Bedding plants are widely available, but the large seeds are so easy to handle that they are often recommended for children's projects. Grow nasturtiums in a soil-based mix amended with sand, and keep the plants in bright sun. Fertilize every two weeks, and pinch off spent blossoms. In hot climates, nasturtiums may be difficult to keep in bloom beyond the middle of summer, though the foliage may remain healthy.

HOW TO USE

Nasturtiums look great planted in a single-species tangle, or can be partnered with bidens or annual baby's breath in more elegant compositions. They are also ideal for mixing with herbs, as both the flowers and leaves of nasturtium are edible.

Nemesia
Nemesia hybrids

Although not well known, nemesias are fantastic flowers to grow in cool spring weather in containers that are viewed up close. The bicolored pocket-book-type flowers, in pink and yellow or red and white, come on in a sudden burst in late spring, and fade within a month. Bedding plants may be difficult to find, but if you are looking for an unusual cool-season container plant that is worth the trouble of growing from seed, try nemesia. Grow in any good potting soil, in at least a half-day of full sun. Fertilize every two weeks. Replace plants with a more heat tolerant flower after the blossoms fade.

Nemesias with calendulas.

HOW TO USE

Nemesias may be enjoyed on their own, clustered so that three plants fill an 8-inch pot. They are fabulous when teamed up with gray-foliage plants such as lamb's-ear or dusty miller. Torenias make good summer replacements.

Nicotiana
Nicotiana hybrids

Commonly known as flowering tobacco, nicotianas now come in white, many shades of pink and even lime green. The trumpet-shaped flowers form on upright spikes. Height ranges from 1 to 3 feet. Dwarf cultivars, sold as bedding plants in late spring, are best for containers. Nicotiana can take full sun but prefers partial shade. The plants adapt to any type of soil, but need regular water and fertilization every two weeks. Snip off old flower spikes to encourage new ones to grow.

HOW TO USE

Dwarf nicotianas look rather stiff on their own, but make excellent upright accent plants in mixed bouquets. Lime

Shade tolerant nicotiana.

green or white nicotiana is wonderful with red salvias or geraniums. Try the pinks or reds with coleus.

Nierembergia
Nierembergia hippomanica

Nierembergia deserves wider use, for the plants form neat self-cleaning mounds of color all summer long. They will grow as short-lived perennials south of Zone 7, though they are usually at their best in their first summer. Flowers are white or light purple, and the plants require very little care. Grow them in full sun or partial shade, in any good soil mix and shelter them from heavy rains when they're at their peak. Following heavy drenchings, the plants need a few days to regain their composure.

HOW TO USE

Nierembergias are great planted alone in broad pots that can be moved about as needed to complement other flowers. Good companions include narrow-leaf zinnias, dwarf cosmos and scaevola.

Nolana
Nolana species

This little morning glory look-alike is an ideal plant for hanging baskets that get plenty of sun. Varieties with blue flowers usually have comely white throats, or you can look for nolanas that bloom pure white. Seeds are generally easier to find than bedding plants. Nolanas do best with a rich but gritty soil mixture that drains quickly. Even so, water them regularly and fertilize every two weeks during the summer. Stems trail about 14 inches, and can be pinched back to keep them tidy. Nolana is one of the annual treasures tailor-made for container life.

HOW TO USE

Nolanas make ideal plants for hanging baskets provided they receive only fleeting shade. Combine blue and white varieties in the same container. You can also use nolana to edge mixed bouquets in large containers.

Pansy
Viola x wittrockiana

The color range of pansies is endless, and includes many with plain faces and others with distinctive dark blotches on the petals. Many newer varieties are hardy to Zone 4, which makes fall planting possible in most areas. Even so, you might want to keep your planted pansy containers in a wagon so you can wheel them into a cold garage or porch during savage weather. Starting with bedding plants will save you ten weeks of growing time. Plant pansies in any potting soil, and begin feeding them every two weeks as soon as they show new growth in spring. When they begin blooming well, move them to a bright, sunny location. From Zone 6 southward, toss out leggy pansies in early summer, for they will never recover their vigor.

HOW TO USE
Pansies are at home in pots, windowboxes and even hanging

Pansies.

Plant pansies and tulips together in fall for a great show in spring.

baskets. They are an ideal companion for tulips and other spring bulbs that are planted in fall and kept cold all winter. Also try planting pansies by themselves in large, low bowl-shaped containers, using contrasting colors such as yellow and blue or orange and purple.

Pentas
Pentas lanceolata

In recent years, pentas has gone from being a houseplant to a popular annual bedding plant in warm climates. The star-shaped flowers develop in clusters, and may be red, pink or lavender. A

Heat tolerant pentas.

tropical perennial, plants grown from either seeds or rooted cuttings are now widely available in late spring. They crave warm weather and plenty of sun, but are otherwise easy to grow. Give pentas a light, well-drained potting mix, and water them often. Fertilize plants and pinch off old flowers every week to ten days. Pentas also make good year-round container plants for warm sunrooms.

HOW TO USE
When pansies and other spring bloomers deteriorate in early summer, replace them with pentas. Lantana, portulaca and narrow-leaf zinnias make good companions and have similar needs for warmth and strong sun.

Petunia
Petunia hybrids

Petunias are mainstays for container gardeners, for they often grow better in containers than they do in beds. This is especially true of fancy large-flowered varieties, which are easily damaged by heavy rains. Bright, sunny spots that are sheltered from rain are ideal. Petunias come in many colors, but the pinks, whites and purples are the best bloomers and most likely to have evening fragrance. Reds can be temperamental. Choose cascading

Pink petunias.

grandiflora petunias or Supertunias for baskets, and stiffer floribunda types for mixed bouquets where you need them to bloom non-stop for a long time. Miniature varieties fit nicely into very small pots and window boxes. Petunias thrive in any good soil mix, and need fertilizing at least every two weeks in the summer. Deadhead petunias as much as possible, and shear back plants in midsummer to promote a heavy flush of new flowers in early fall.

HOW TO USE
Petunias combine beautifully with geraniums and many small-flowered summer annuals, including sweet alyssum, bidens, lobelia and verbena. White and pale pink varieties are ideal for bringing grace and unity to all container gardens.

Phlox
Phlox drummondii

Within the large plant genus known as phlox, the best choices for containers are the annuals, commonly called drummond phlox, which are easy to find as bedding plants in early spring. Flowers may be pink, yellow, red or almost blue, with many shades in between. Most are true dwarfs that grow to only eight inches tall. Drummond phlox grows best in cool weather, and tends to decline quickly when summer comes to warmer climates. In Zones 9 and 10, grow this flower from fall to spring. Regardless of season, drummond phlox needs good sun, a rich soilless potting mix and fertilizer every two weeks. Deadhead plants often to keep new flowers coming.

HOW TO USE
Individual phlox plants in small pots have a distinctively dainty demeanor. Use these plants in mixed bouquets only in cool summer climates where they are likely to bloom for a long time. They work well with blue forget-me-nots or lacy white sweet alyssum.

Polka dot plant
Hypoestes phyllostachya

Polka dot plant can live for years as a houseplant, or you can buy bedding plants in spring and grow them as summer annuals in a shady outdoor location. These plants rarely bloom, and are grown for their unusual pink or white variegated foliage. Grow in a sterile soilless mix and pinch back stems monthly to encourage bushy growth. Fertilize lightly every two to three weeks.

HOW TO USE
If your main flowers for shade are pale pink or white impatiens, you will find their ideal partners in pink polka dot plants. Plant your polka dots in their own containers so you can shift them around to help spotlight other plantings. One plant will quickly fill an 8-inch pot, or you can place two or three plants in a wider, urn-shaped container.

Portulaca
Portulaca grandiflora

Also known as moss rose, portulacas are warm-weather annuals that grow to only 6 inches tall, yet spread outward at least a foot when grown in strong sun. The bright yellow, orange, pink or white flowers resemble small roses, and the foliage is succulent in nature. Buy bedding plants in late spring, or sow seeds outdoors after the weather has warmed in early summer. Flowers usually close at night. While open during the day, they are often visited by honeybees. Plant portulacas in a sandy soil mixture, in broad dishes that accentuate their spread. Although quite drought tolerant, portulacas grow best with regular water and fertilizer.

HOW TO USE
When grown alone in low containers, portulacas create a ground cover effect. They are perfect for planting beneath taller roses, and make nice companions for large cacti, as well.

Salvia
Salvia species

The salvias grown as summer annuals include three different species. The most common are *Salvia splendens* varieties, which produce upright spikes of tubular red, white or blue flowers atop bushy plants. The red shades are usually the strongest growers, especially in partial shade. Another good species increasingly available as bedding plants, *Salvia coccinea*, is a thrifty, upright plant that's great for adding spikes of coral or red to mixed

Phlox.

Polka dot plant.

Salvia coccinea *(upper left) and blue sage (upper right) bring welcome vertical strength to container bouquets.*

bouquets that get plenty of sun. A third summer salvia, *S. farinacea*, is known as blue salvia or mealycup sage. It grows as a perennial south of Zone 7. The slender blue spikes are so useful in mixed bouquets that few container gardeners can go a season without them. All salvias like a rich potting mix and regular water and fertilizer. Deadhead promptly to promote the growth of new blossoms.

HOW TO USE

Bold red *S. splendens* are at their best when accompanied by soft gray foliage plants such as dusty miller. *S. coccinea* is a good annual to mix with floppy summer annuals like bidens or cosmos, or perennial coreopsis and rudbeckia. *Salvia farinacea* glows when accompanied by silvery artemisias, and mixes beautifully with almost any shade of geranium.

NOTE Hardy perennial sage species are described on page 84, among perennials, and on page 106, among herbs.

Sanvitalia
Sanvitalia procumbens

This spreading annual looks like a petite creeping zinnia, though the small orange or yellow flowers invariably have dark purplish-brown centers. Some garden centers carry bedding plants, but you may need to start your own seeds in late spring. Sanvitalia grows only 4 to 6 inches tall, but stems trail outward more than a

Orange-yellow sanvitalia.

foot. Plants need dry conditions and strong sun, and benefit from regular water and fertilizer every two to three weeks.

HOW TO USE

Sanvitalia is a nice change of pace for containers that receive substantial sun. It is great in hanging baskets, or you can let the stems spill over the edges or large containers.

Scaevola
Scaevola species

Also known as fan plant, cool blue scaevola is quickly becoming a favorite flower among container gardeners. Actually a tender perennial, you will probably have no problem finding rooted cuttings sold in small pots at garden centers in late spring. Individual scaevola plants grow to about 1 foot tall and 2 feet wide, and stay covered with blue blossoms all summer. They are at their best in full sun, and are amazingly tolerant of extreme heat. Plant scaevola in any quality potting

Scaevola.

soil, and fertilize only every three to four weeks. Deadheading is seldom necessary, but you can shear back large plants in late summer to renew their vigor.

HOW TO USE

Scaevola is so showy on its own that you will probably want to showcase a trio of plants in a large pot kept on a sunny deck or patio. It also grows well in roomy baskets or wall planters. Good companions include artemisias and color-coordinated petunias.

Scarlet runner bean
Phaseolus species

The most ornamental of beans, scarlet runners produce small clusters of bright red blossoms on 6- to 8-foot twining vines. A dwarf cultivar, 'Scarlet Bees', is almost compact as a bush snap bean. Scarlet runner beans need sun and a heavy, soil-based potting mix and the vining strains need support as they run. After your last spring frost has passed, plant seeds directly in large containers. The young pods are edible, like snap beans, but quickly become tough as they age. Pick them anyway to promote prolonged flowering.

Scarlet runner bean.

HOW TO USE

Grow long-vined scarlet runners in a roomy wood or plastic box set on the ground, or use a large 12-inch pot. Train the vines up a chain fence or string trellis. Scarlet runners make a great summer shade screen. Use 'Scarlet Bees' in mixed container bouquets with yellow cosmos, marigolds or nasturtiums.

Schizanthus
Schizanthus pinnatus

Commonly known as butterfly flower, schizanthus grows best where nights remain cool. The showy flowers resemble little orchids, and each petal is usually splashed with several shades of pink or lilac. The bushy plants grow to about 15 inches tall and are at their best in filtered shade. They will also bloom when brought indoors and kept in good light. Buy bedding plants in early spring, for schizanthus is very slow to start from seed. Use any good quality potting soil, and fertilize every three weeks. Deadhead to promote steady blooming.

HOW TO USE

Since they like filtered shade, schizanthus is a good annual to plug into the soil beneath potted trees or open shrubs. Keep a few plants in separate pots so you can enjoy them indoors during the winter.

Snapdragon
Antirrhinum majus

Naturally neat snapdragons can be found in a rainbow of sunny colors, including yellow, red and pink. Very tall varieties are easily toppled by wind, and even intermediate-sized snaps may need slender stakes to hold them upright. Little dwarfs, only 8 to 10 inches high, need no support and do well in sunny planters and window boxes. Bedding plants are often available in fall from Zone 6 southward, where they are usually winter hardy. In other areas, plant early in the spring. Use a rich potting mix and fertilize every two weeks. Pinch back the first spike that forms on young plants to promote the development of multiple flowering spikes. When your snaps are in full flower, clip off faded flower spikes every week.

HOW TO USE

Intermediate-size snapdragons make fine upright accents in mixed bouquets with other cool-natured annuals such as sweet alyssum, lobelia and nemesia. In windowboxes, tone down the formal posture of snaps by edging boxes with sweet alyssum or tendrils of vinca major.

Stock
Matthiola incana

Stocks are some of the most fragrant annuals you can grow in containers. Plants that bear white flowers are usually the strongest growers, but you may find bedding plants in red or pink, too. Stocks need good sun and plenty of cool weather, yet they cannot tolerate frost. Stocks are slow but steady growers when started from seed in late winter. Choose dwarf cultivars for containers, and give them a rich soil mix that retains moisture well. Dispose of plants in summer after daytime temperatures reach the 90s, for they will quickly decline.

HOW TO USE

Since few climates are just right for prolonged performance from stocks, grow them in their own pots, and move them to the close quarters of outdoor living areas when they are in full bloom.

Sunflower
Helianthus annuus

In recent years, plant breeders have developed new sunflowers that grow to less than 3 feet tall. These dwarf sunflowers are dazzling when grown in pots kept on a sunny deck or patio. When in flower, expect the blossoms to face south, where sunlight is most intense. Sow seeds in well weighted pots in late spring, and cover with folded newspapers for a few days if needed to keep the soil constantly moist. Begin fertilizing lightly every

Schizanthus, or butterfly flower.

Dwarf sunflowers.

two weeks after the plants are 6 inches tall. Clip off the first flowers as soon as they have peaked to promote the development of new flowering branches.

HOW TO USE

Grow dwarf sunflowers in their own containers, for their extensive fibrous root system will crowd out those of other plants. Use your sunflower pot as a central element in a grouping with other bright bloomers. After the last flowers fade, set the pots where goldfinches and other birds can collect the seeds.

Sweet pea
Lathyrus odoratus

Sweet peas flourish in climates where cool spring weather stretches well into summer, and they begin to suffer when temperatures rise above the mid-80s. Purple and mauve varieties are reliably strong bloomers, often with good fragrance. Plant sweet peas early, while frost still lingers. Before planting the seeds 2 inches deep in a tall, heavy pot, fashion a trellis for them. Eight straight but shapely tree branches, pushed into the soil inside the rim of the pot and bound together

at the top with twine is ideal. Sweet peas cling with curly tendrils, but still may need occasional tying up. Fertilize sweet peas early and often with a weak liquid solution. If needed, spray with a stream of cold water or use insecticidal soap to control pea aphids.

HOW TO USE

Grow sweet pea vines by themselves and use the container and trellis as a vertical accent in your container garden. When flowering stops, discard plants and re-use the soil for a flower other than sweet peas.

Torenia
Torenia species

Also called wishbone flower, torenia is as easy to grow as impatiens, but the plants can take a bit more sun. The 10-inch plants produce blue or pink flowers with lighter colored throats. Bushy and compact, torenia requires little care beyond plenty of water and fertilizer every two weeks. Look for bedding plants in late spring, and snap them up before they are gone. This flower is at its best during the warm days of midsummer, and usually stays in bloom all the way to frost.

HOW TO USE

Try pairing torenia with white nicotiana, or with coleus selections with chartreuse leaves. Pink or white polka dot plants also make colorful companions.

Verbena
Verbena hybrids

Annual verbenas produce rounded clusters of flowers in early summer, in soft pastels or bold pink, purple, white and red. They grow to only 8 inches tall and spread sideways into loose mounds. Get bedding plants situated early, for they like cool weather. Full sun is best, but you will get a more relaxed growing habit when plants grow in afternoon shade. Provide a rich, quick-draining soil mix, and fertilize every three weeks up until plants flower. Thereafter, fertilize lightly after deadheading every 10 days or so. In warm climates, annual verbena usually flowers well only until midsummer.

HOW TO USE

The light peach 'Peaches and Cream' cultivar brings an airy touch to compositions made up of herbs and

Dwarf sweet peas.

Orange, yellow and purple nemesia dance within a bounteous hanging basket.

A mound of pink moss verbena.

Pink garden zinnias.

White vincas make quiet company for a wide variety of plants.

foliage plants. Pair scarlet red verbena with mealycup sage (*Salvia farinacea*), or let purple-flowered selections mingle with white geraniums or petunias.

Vinca
Catharanthus roseus

Truly a low-maintenance flower, annual vinca asks only for warm temperatures and at least a half day of sun. Also known as Madagascar periwinkle, the older white varieties (with red central eyes) have given way to more elegant selections that may be soft pastel pink, pale lavender or nearly irridescent pink. The 12-inch plants grow upright at first, and then spread into thick mounds. Set bedding plants in containers filled with any good soil mix, and fertilize monthly unless the plants seem to lack vigor. Dump the used soil and scrub out pots at the end of the season, for vincas sometimes host a persistent root fungus.

HOW TO USE
Annual vincas make ideal summer replacements for cool-season flowers. You can also plant them over spring-flowering bulbs, or alongside upright cannas. In container bouquets, yellow plume celosia or yellow gem marigolds make fine companions.

Zinnia
Zinnia species

Two species of zinnia make good container subjects for summer. The familiar garden zinnia, *Z. elegans*, is a rather stiff, upright plant available in a huge assortment of sizes, colors and flower forms. Narrowleaf zinnia, *Z. angustifolia*, is a more spreading plant that produces orange or white flowers. A new zinnia cultivar worth trying in containers is called 'Pinwheel'. It combines the characteristics of the two species, producing white and pink single flowers. All zinnias may be easily started from seed, or you can buy bedding plants. Avoid crowding them

in pots, for they need plenty of light and fresh air to grow well. A sandy soil mix is preferred, accompanied by light fertilization every two weeks. Dead-head often to keep new flowers coming.

HOW TO USE
Old-fashioned garden zinnias have a coarse texture that tends to dominate other plants. You can soften their appearance by choosing light pink or yellow colors, accompanied by gray foliage plants like dusty miller. Narrowleaf zinnias combine well with numerous summer annuals, or you can let two or three plants turn a 10-inch pot into a mass of sunny color.

Disease resistant narrow-leaf zinnias.

Chapter 6

❧

PERSISTENT PERENNIALS

erennials, that vital group of long-lasting, nonwoody plants, grow for years in the same container, giving you both beautiful flowers and interesting foliage. Designing with perennials is satisfying because they come back every year, usually following a period of winter dormancy, and grow to about the same size they were the year before. You can grow perennials in mixed container bouquets with annuals, herbs or shrubs, or use them alone to make strong textural statements. For example, you might mix coreopsis, ivy or trailing periwinkle with a wide range of blooming annuals. Other perennials, including broad-leafed hosta and stately foxglove, are at their best when allowed to fill planters by themselves.

The most rugged of perennials are terrific for solving difficult landscaping problems. Set containers of daylily or

Profusely blooming perennials stage a patio party, including coreopsis, yellow gerbera daisies, white shasta daisies, gaillardia and rudbeckia.

liriope on top of hot pavement. Ivy, ferns or hostas in containers can help bring shady areas to life, including spots that are so filled with tree roots that digging the ground is impossible. Trailing ivy and periwinkle are unmatched for gracing the edges of window boxes or tall containers, and the cool gray foliage of artemisias helps unify riotous groupings of your brightest summer bloomers. Many more specific ideas for using perennials in container gardens are described in the profiles later in this chapter.

Some perennials are grown for their flowers, some for their foliage and some for both. In container gardening, foliage can be more important than flowers, and there is quite an array of foliage color and texture to choose from among cultivars of ivy, artemisia, coral bells and liriope. These and some other perennials are nearly evergreen, even in very cold climates.

Most hardy perennials bloom magnificently once a year, usually at a predictable time. The bloom time of some perennials is quite limited, but that

should not stop you from including them in your container garden. For example, candytuft becomes a cloud of white blossoms for a few short weeks in late spring, but is among the best flowering-groundcover-type plants for the edges of containers planted with bulbs, shrubs, trees or tall upright perennials. And no flower can match the dazzling fall display put on by chrysanthemums. In general, hardy perennials that produce daisy-like flowers (rudbeckia, coreopsis) tend to bloom a little longer than others, especially if you trim off

Long-blooming geraniums must be kept indoors through winter. In spring, move them indoors into the colorful company of summer annuals.

the old blossoms promptly to make way for the new. The longest bloom times come from frost-tender perennials like fuchsia and geranium (*Pelargonium* species). These plants bloom continuously until they are damaged by freezing weather. Before this can happen, bring them indoors to enjoy as flowering houseplants.

Wherever you live, you can use perennials to stretch the seasons beyond their usual boundaries. Jazz up your summer terraces with tropical bougainvillea, and bring the plant indoors for winter, putting a heavy pot on casters if necessary. In warm climates, use the opposite approach and bring cool-weather plants like violas indoors into an air conditioned room to enjoy a few more weeks of bloom.

PERENNIALS IN POTS

Since most perennials have no trouble surviving cold winter weather when left outdoors, choose frostproof containers unless you live in Zone 9 or 10. Terracotta pots will crack open when the soil inside them freezes hard, which will leave you with the task of repotting plants in bone-numbing cold. Plastic, fiberglass, cement and wood containers do a better job of holding up to freezing conditions.

You can start some perennials from seed, but it often takes two years for a seedling to grow large enough to bloom well. You can save much time and often get superior plants by starting with purchased plants. In nurseries, most perennials are propagated from stem cuttings or root divisions, so the new plant is exactly like its parent in terms of color, shape and size. Most of the best strains of perennials are propagated this way. At the same time, some perennials are so easy to start from seed that they are worth the wait, especially if you live where winters are mild. In Zones 7 and 8, for example, you can start seeds of candytuft and coreopsis in early fall, and the plants will bloom beautifully the following spring. See page 52 for basic seed starting instructions.

Grow a diverse collection of perennial plants by providing the type of soil they prefer: moist, dry, gritty, rich, limy or acid (see pages 31 to 32 for details on these soil types). Also take sun, wind and other site factors into consideration until you get to know each perennial you adopt as an individual. If a plant does not seem to like where you have placed it, try it in a new spot. You will often find that plants with leaves that are narrow, hairy or fleshy can take harsh sun, drought, and drying wind, while those with soft, thin leaves tend to prefer sheltered shade and constant moisture.

PROPAGATING PERENNIALS

Nursery professionals have no monopoly on the propagation of perennials. Learning to start plants from divisions and cuttings makes container gardening with perennials even more satisfying. Besides propagating your own plants, you can use starter divisions or stem cuttings from plants that belong to friends and relatives—a sentimental undertaking that can also be a great money saver.

Timing can be critical when you are propagating plants. In most areas, early spring and late fall are the best times to turn one plant into many smaller ones. In frost-free regions, propagate during moist weather or at the time of year that new growth begins. A cloudy day or late afternoon is best, for transplants are under less water stress when they are not in the sun. By the way, keep the pieces cool, shaded and moist while you are working. Damp newspaper or paper towels are fine for this purpose. After setting the starter divisions and cuttings in their new containers, keep them shaded and well watered until they adjust to life on their own, then move them to their normal conditions.

Before you begin, examine the roots of the plant you want to divide. Most perennials and bulbs can be propagated in one or more of the four ways described here. Some of these instructions also apply to shrubs, vines, annuals, herbs and vegetables. Special propagating directions are included in some of the plant entries that follow.

CROWN DIVISION Are there many small but separately rooted plants or bulbs? This is often the case with chrysanthemums, ferns, daylilies and other clump-forming perennials. Pull the whole clump from the container and separate the plants with your fingers or two planting forks. Sometimes the plants are so interconnected that you must use a sharp knife to cut the clump into separate crowns with visible roots on each piece. Replant the divisions into a sterile soilless mix in clean nursery pots or directly into container bouquets. If you are dealing with bulbs, divide them while they are dormant.

Plants to propagate this way:
achillea
agapanthus
alliums
artemisia
bergenia
candytuft (perennial)
chives
clivia
coreopsis
crocus
daffodil
daylily
fern
gladiolus
grape hyacinth
hyacinth
irises, bulbous
ivy
liriope
mint
primula
saxifrage
sedum
snowdrop
vinca major, vinca minor

ROOT DIVISION Is there a big, tough root mass with several plants coming out of it from separate crowns (central rosettes of leaves)? Hostas often grow this way, and the best way to divide them is with a large, sharp knife, choosing spots between the leafy crowns and slicing straight down through the thick roots. This will seem drastic but the plants will survive if you don't make the sections too small. If in doubt, just cut the mass in half. If you are braver and the clump is large, cut it into quarters. Then replant the pieces immediately, as with crown divisions.

Or are the roots less tough and woody, but thick and branched in a complicated way? Plants from rhizomes such as cannas and bearded iris are like this. Cut through the thick part of the root in a way that gives you one or more new plants or eyes on each piece, preferably with some feeder roots attached.

Plants to propagate this way:
bearded iris
bergenia
canna
coral bells
hosta
iris
mint
most grasses

STEM CUTTINGS Savvy gardeners know how to root a new plant from just a small piece of something they covet. By taking cuttings, you can protect starts of your favorite plants from freezing even if there is no space to bring in the whole pot. You can grow many kinds of perennials, tropical annuals, vines and shrubs this way, but not true bulbs. Some plants such as coleus and ivy are easier or faster to root than others. In fact, some are so easy they will root in a glass of plain water on a windowsill.

Cut pieces about 4 to 6 inches long of new growth (tip growth is preferred).

Dip the bottom cut end into water and then into rooting hormone (available at garden centers, usually as a white powder). Several products are available, and may include fungicide along with the hormone. Insert the bottom half of each cutting into a pot or flat of clean potting soil. Keep the containers moist and shaded, in constant mild temperature, under fluorescent light or in shade.

In a few weeks to a few months, the cuttings will take root. Start more than you need, for usually some will take and some won't. Do not disturb the cuttings until a sizable root mass has grown. Then transplant the cutting, handling it like the plant divisions already mentioned.

Plants to propagate this way:
(easiest and fastest types)
basil
begonia
bougainvillea
chrysanthemum
coleus
fuchsia
geranium
hydrangea
ivy
salvia
sedum
sweet potato
tomato
vinca vine

CARING FOR PERENNIALS IN CONTAINERS

Plants in containers are dependent on you for water and nutrients, so check them every day and water and fertilize them according to their needs. Groom plants regularly by snipping off yellowed leaves and spent flowers. Watch for overcrowding, too. If your container plants perk up when you water but wilt a few hours later, there are too many roots filling the pot, and you should thin the plants or move them all to a larger pot. Non-hardy perennials can be moved indoors in winter and placed outdoors again after the danger of frost passes. In borderline areas such as Zone 9, back up your tender perennials such as geraniums and bougainvillea with cuttings if frost is expected and you are unable to move the pots. Some gardeners in mild winter areas keep a list of their tender plants handy so that they can quickly gather them together to protect them from frost.

KEEPING DORMANT PERENNIALS THROUGH WINTER

Tender perennials can be kept in their pots and grown another year if you have a frost-free place to store them. Experienced gardeners often find ways to transport large pots on casters into their favorite protective spots. A garage, laundry room, cool basement or sunroom may offer just the shelter you need.

Geraniums (*Pelargonium* species), for example, tolerate very little frost but benefit from a rest or dormant period. To take advantage of this, cut the plants back in the fall by about half. Let the soil and foliage dry out for a few days and then move the pot into a cool area that does not get bright light. Let the soil stay fairly but not completely dry. Add water sparingly from time to time. Remove foliage as it browns or wilts. After two months of rest, bring the pots into more light and resume watering and feeding. As soon as there is no danger of frost, put the pots outside again, gradually acclimating the plants by moving them out for only a few hours at a time at first. By now, new growth should be luxuriant. Other semi-hardy plants can be handled similarly, including begonia, New Zealand flax, fuchsia, verbena and a number of bulbs.

A Gallery of Perennials

There is no limit to the kinds of perennials you can use in pots and containers if you provide the right conditions. Here are 35 popular choices to use by themselves or in combination with other plants. Each entry includes common and botanical names, hardiness zones, description, basic needs and an interesting planting idea.

Achillea, Yarrow
Achillea millefolium
Zones 2 to 8

With fernlike foliage and large, flat-topped clusters of summer flowers in white and pastel shades of yellow, peach and red, this easy-going plant also attracts butterflies. Yarrow looks delicate but is rugged, preferring full sun. Like most wildflowers, it grows better in rich, well-drained soil, but can take neglect and still prosper. Since fernleaf yarrow can grow too enthusiastically, this is a good plant to keep in containers rather than having it get away from you in the garden. After blooms fade, deadhead by cutting down the flower stalks near the base of the plant. The best colors are available as plants propagated by crown division. Divide clumps every other year in spring or fall; transplant to broad frostproof containers.

PLANTING IDEA In fall, combine fresh divisions with spring-blooming bulbs such as hyacinths, tulips or daffodils planted below them. The yarrow will bloom after the bulbs finish.

Agapanthus, Lily of the Nile
Agapanthus species
Grows in all zones, with frost protection.

Here is a stately flower with ball-shaped clusters of tubular flowers on 2-foot stems, with equally attractive straplike green leaves. Flower color ranges from deep blue to white. Agapanthus likes crowded conditions in rich, moist, sandy soil that is well-drained, with full sun. It is marginally cold hardy. Most varieties are safe without protection in Zones 8 to 11. 'Headbourne Hybrids', including deep blue 'Bressingham Blue', are the hardiest, and can be grown outdoors in Zones 6 to 9. In all zones, agapanthus can be grown in large tubs and brought into a cool basement or sunroom for winter. Plants are usually grown by themselves in containers, for the roots do not leave room for competitors. Divide the plants in spring every few years or if flower quality declines.

PLANTING IDEA Use agapanthus to structure your container garden's design, for it has a unique, clean texture that evokes a tropical mood.

This plant is ideal for filling long, rectangular planters, or you can use one large pot as a focal point.

Alyssum, Basket of Gold
Aurinia saxatilis
Zones 3 to 7

Making a scented golden wave of small flowers on plants under a foot tall but two or three times as wide, basket of gold alyssum is a dazzler in early to mid-spring. Very easy to grow, this is a finely textured cascading plant that looks fantastic when encouraged to drape over container edges. Cut the plants back after they flower. Propagate basal stem cuttings in late winter or fall to keep plants going. Gold alyssum (which is different from sweet alyssum, an annual) likes slightly acidic, well-drained soil. Tall containers or window boxes that need a cascading edging plant are good showcases for this easy perennial.

PLANTING IDEA Combine basket of gold with tulips, azalea or spring phlox. Retire containers to an out-of-the-way place after the blooms are gone.

Artemisia
Artemisia species
Zones 4 to 9, most species

Silver contrasts are lovely in mixed containers, so you are sure to find many places for artemisias, a large group of plants with aromatic, delicate silver foliage. These plants tolerate sun, wind and dry soil and are nearly or completely evergreen, depending on climate. Some are good seaside plants. Dwarf types are usually best for pots because tall plants can be leggy, especially if grown in too much shade. Aromatic *A. arborescens*, fine-leaved and silvery, is hardy only to Zone 8. *A. absinthium* gives a similar misty effect and is hardy through Zone 6. *A. ludoviciana* ('Silver Queen' and 'Silver King') is coarser in texture but hardy to Zone 5, and has bright, nearly white

Achillea with sweet alyssum.

Agapanthus.

foliage. *A. lactiflora* (white mugwort) blooms in summer and fall with large sprays of white flowers. There are many other species and named cultivars. Provide a well-drained potting mixture of average fertility and an open, sunny site. Trim back in spring and prune for shape as needed. Propagate artemisias by rooting stem cuttings taken in spring or early fall.

PLANTING IDEA Place pots on pedestals with ivy trailing downward and a frothy planting of *Artemisia lactiflora* taking center stage. Plug small rooted cuttings into mixed container bouquets.

Bergenia
Bergenia species
Zones 3 to 8

These hardy evergreen perennials have round, cabbagey looking, leathery leaves about a foot tall which make a nice contrast with bulbs. Purple or pink waxy flowers appear on spires in late winter and spring. Provide a well-drained potting mix, not too rich and not too dry. A sunny site is fine if plants don't get too hot, but give them more shade in the South. Keep plants well-groomed by removing damaged leaves, especially after winter ends.

PLANTING IDEA Surround boldly textured bergenia with a low-growing planting of strawberry begonia (*Saxifraga stolonifera*) or any light-textured annual.

Bougainvillea
Bougainvillea hybrids
Zones 9 to 11, other areas with frost protection

This showy tropical vine features masses of flowers (actually long-lasting papery bracts) in hot shades of pink, red, orange and purple. Growing it in containers limits its size somewhat, but that's all right because otherwise it can reach the top of a two story building.

Bougainvillea.

Leaves are heart shaped, and, in time, canes become woody and thorny. Since they are fairly salt tolerant, bougainvilleas are often used near the sea. Keep the soil rich and on the acid side. Provide plenty of pot space for this vigorous and spectacular plant. Never let it freeze. Train bougainvillea onto supports or let it drape from a hanging basket, pruning it often to keep it shapely.

PLANTING IDEA Set containers of bougainvillea atop a wall or attach hooks and hang them in filtered sun. Let plants cascade in a mass of color.

Candytuft
Iberis sempervirens
Zones 4 to 9

Candytuft is a mat-forming evergreen plant, 8 inches tall, that succeeds in well-drained containers in full sun. Plants cover themselves with thousands of small white flowers in spring. Cut them back to 2 to 3 inches tall after flowering ends to keep them neat and to promote new growth. Drainage is important to prevent root rot. In mid- to late summer, make divisions from basal stem cuttings.

PLANTING IDEA Use at the outer edge of pots and planters, letting the flowers and foliage drape down gracefully.

Carnation, Florist's
Dianthus caryophyllus
Zones 8 to 10

Carnations are pot plants which can be grown from seed or cuttings. In cold-winter areas, start seeds in December for flowers the same year. In mild-winter areas that do not get too hot, you may use them as perennials. Color and size vary, but many types, including 'Chabaud' and 'Burpee's Super Giants' are about 18 inches tall in bloom. Pot size should be 8 or more inches wide. Provide well-drained, fertile, slightly alkaline soil, and grow them in cool weather. Stake and deadhead as needed.

PLANTING IDEA Carnations were chosen in 1907 as the emblem of Mother's Day, so they make a perfect gift on that occasion, blooming in an attractive container.

Chrysanthemum
Dendranthema hybrids
Zones 4 to 11

Chrysanthemums bloom in what are known as fall colors—yellow, gold, wine, bronze, white and lavender—and put on a magnificent show in autumn.

Cascading chrysanthemum.

In Zones 7 to 10 certain types bloom twice a year. Plant size ranges from 6 or 8 inches to several feet tall, and flower sizes and shapes range from tiny buttons or daisies to "football" mums with 6-inch heads. All forms do well in pots, and should be kept evenly moist and fertilized monthly. Plant chrysanthemums in full sun in a rich but well-drained potting mixture. Pinch back stems every three weeks until the end of June to make plants bushier. Cut back flowers after they fade. In spring, dig and divide the stoloniferous roots (runners) when new growth begins, every year or two. You can also root stem cuttings taken in early spring.

PLANTING IDEA Pot up runners of chrysanthemums in individual 8-inch pots in spring and grow them in an out-of-the-way place until August. Then use them to replace fading annuals in your planters.

Clematis
Clematis species
Zones 4 to 8

In regions where it is hardy, you will see a lot of clematis, for it is one of the world's most beautiful flowering vines. Colors range from white through pink, rose, red and purple, including many intense shades. Large-flowered types such as 'Jackmanii' have flat-faced flowers 4 or more inches wide. Flowers can be single or double depending on the cultivar, and either spring blooming or repeat flowering. Species clematis may be bell shaped. All clematis vines climb ingenuously by twining their leaves around supports, so plant them in large containers and provide a structure on which to train them. Mature vines can grow upward over 25 feet but may instead be wound around lower, wider frames. Preferred soil is moist, rich, and lightly laced with lime. Plants prefer shade in the root zone but more sun for leaves and flowers.

Clematis.

PLANTING IDEA Use clematis topiary for an entranceway. Place two cube-shaped wooden planters about 30 inches wide on either side of the door, each holding a clematis vine trained onto a 4-foot, conical frame.

Clivia, Kaffir Lily
Clivia miniata
All zones, with frost protection

In areas with cold winters, clivia is perfect for big containers that stay in a brightly sunlit room until the danger of frost passes, then spend summer

Clivia.

outdoors on a deck or patio. In Zones 9 to 11, clivia is hardy outdoors in partial shade. Clivia is related to amaryllis (a bulb), but it is easier to grow. Broad green straplike leaves up to 2 feet long and 3 inches wide are ever-green. Large lily-like orange flowers appear in

Clivia.

clusters on a strong scape (stem-like portion). They usually bloom in spring, but bloom time varies with climate. When thick roots multiply and side shoots form, move the plant cluster to a larger planter or tub. Clivia looks best when five or more plants are blooming together. When a cluster outgrows its pot, make root divisions to separate and thin the plants.

PLANTING IDEA Grow a cluster of clivia in a handsome tub for a spectacular accent.

Coral Bells
Heuchera species
Zones 3 to 9

Native to much of North America, coral bells is winter hardy, blooms from spring to fall and is nearly evergreen. The wild form usually has green leaves and long-lasting plumes of small, red-coral flowers in summer, but there are many hybrids with bronze, silvery purple or reddish foliage. Flowers can be white, pink or red, 12 to 24 inches tall, and sometimes are fragrant. Forms with colorful purple foliage combine well with other plants. All types prefer moist but well-drained potting soil and a semi-shady or shady site. Do not allow soil to dry out completely. Divide crowns every three years, preferably in early spring.

PLANTING IDEA Plant a 36-inch frost-proof container with six plants of a red or purple-leafed cultivar of coral bells. Border it with an outer row of periwinkle vine and add some pink sweet alyssum to trail over the edges of the pot.

Coreopsis
Coreopsis species
Zones 4 to 9

This group of sun-loving perennials is easy to grow and features cheerful, daisylike free-blooming flowers during the hottest part of summer. *Coreopsis lanceolata* is native to the eastern half of the United States, but short-stemmed or dwarf types need no staking and are better for containers. The root ball of coreopsis is not especially large, so it's a good mixer. Divide clumps in the fall by cutting crowns into individual rosettes, which develop new roots very quickly. Plants are also easily grown from seed. Coreopsis prefers well drained, slightly gritty soil, but will grow in almost any soil provided it gets good sun.

PLANTING IDEA Fill a big basket, about 30 inches wide and 20 inches deep, with a waterproof plastic liner with several drainage holes. Fill with rich but sandy potting soil and plant with dwarf yellow coreopsis such as 'Domino', white petunias, and woolly lamb's-ear for a sparkling gold, silver and white combination.

Daylily
Hemerocallis species
Zones 3 to 9

Busy daylily breeders have given us endless choices, with plants ranging from 1 to 4 feet in height and in every conceivable color except blue and pure white. The leaves are grasslike and are evergreen to Zone 9. Plants prefer full

Daylily.

sun or bright partial shade, and have few pests. Clumps send up several stiff stems bearing a cluster of lily-like flowers, with one or two opening at a time. Each blossom lasts only a day (the flower symbolizes flirting in Victorian flower language). The succession of buds opens for a month or more, though dwarf everblooming varieties bloom off and on all summer. Divide plants in fall or early spring by pulling clumps apart and replanting the crowns.

PLANTING IDEA Everblooming types such as 'Stella D'Oro', 'Pardon Me' and 'Happy Returns' are best for pots and tubs.

English Ivy
Hedera helix
Zones 5 to 9

"Tell me why the ivy twines," go the words of an old song. Ivy is a very tough, hardy evergreen vine that grows in almost any light, even full shade, clinging with hairlike feeder roots to climb up any nearby surface. Any soil is satisfactory if it is well drained.

English ivy.

Water and fertilize moderately. In containers, ivy trails very attractively from the front or sides, combining well with upright plants such as shrubs or geraniums. Or it can climb buildings or supports to make a strong feature in a small garden space. It has lush foliage which can be light or dark green or variegated with white, yellow or rusty colors. Ivy is easily propagated by rooting cuttings taken from the growing tips. This plant is so versatile and useful that you will probably want to root a collection of cuttings every spring and fall so you will always have them on hand for plugging into other containers.

PLANTING IDEA Make an ivy topiary by making or buying a wire form lined with sphagnum moss. Set it in a large container planted with several long, rooted cuttings of ivy, and weave the ivy in and out of the form until all parts are covered. Continue training and weaving as the ivy grows. Water and fertilize often to promote faster growth and better coverage of the topiary form. When it is finished, maintain it with frequent grooming and pruning.

Fern
Many genera and species
Types for all zones

There are super ferns for all climates, and they all can be grown in containers if light and soil conditions are suitable. Ferns usually grow in moist, peaty potting soil in partial shade. Attractive foliage is usually green but may be lighter, darker or touched with silver or bronze. Size ranges from about 6 inches to several feet tall, with most types about 16 inches tall. Look for evergreen ferns for permanent pots. Christmas fern is good in northern zones and Boston and leather fern may be used in Zones 9 and 10. Fertilize ferns monthly with weak fish emulsion or other water soluble fertilizer, for they are easily damaged by harsh chemical fertilizers.

Ferns grace an uptown terrace.

PLANTING IDEA Small offshoots or crown divisions from ferns from your garden can be used in a disposable fashion to mix with impatiens and other shade-tolerant plants in bouquet-style containers.

Flax, New Zealand
Phormium tenax
Zones 7 to 9

Trim yet bold, New Zealand flax with its pointed straplike leaves about 2 feet long makes a lively container companion or solo performer. It is a semi-hardy evergreen which may have green, bronze or variegated leaves. New Zealand flax is tough enough for sites exposed to wind in either a sunny or partially shaded site. It prefers moist but well-drained soil and cool summers.

PLANTING IDEA In partial shade, set a large urn on a pedestal base. Fill it with the New Zealand flax pointing upward, coleus in a coordinated color billowing sideways and ivy or periwinkle vine trailing downward.

Foxglove
Digitalis species
Zones 3 to 8

Foxgloves provide stately spires of 2- to 3-inch bell-shaped flowers and are striking when used in containers. The flowers open from bottom to top, with stems elongating as flowers emerge. Plants need partial shade, rich loamy soil, and a generous allotment of space

Upright foxglove, Digitalis purpurea.

common name, lady's eardrops. Colors are mainly pink, red, purple and white, and attract hummingbirds from far away. Fuchsia is a tender perennial that is often treated as an annual. If protected from frost, it can be maintained for years. Keep plants in a warm place in winter, and cut back in early spring to promote side shoots. Provide a moist, rich, but well-drained potting mixture and a sheltered, semi-shady or shady spot. Fertilize lightly every two weeks in summer. If you must water your fuchsia more than once a day in warm weather, the containers are probably too small.

PLANTING IDEA Treat your balcony, deck or terrace to a very large raised planter or tub of fuchsia. If protected from heavy rains, you will be amazed at the luxuriant growth your plants make when they have fertile soil and plenty of space and moisture.

Geranium
Pelargonium species
Zones 9 to 11, other regions with
   protection

With good care, geraniums bloom vividly all summer with clusters of flowers in shades of white, pink, coral, violet and red. They are tender perennials from South Africa, often cultivated as annuals. There is a wide choice of color and form in both flower and leaf. In bloom, plant size ranges from about

for roots. Colors range from white through peach, pink, violet and purple, usually dotted with brown spots. The white form is exquisite against a dark hedge. Remove the top two-thirds of the flower spike after the blossoms begin to fade to encourage reblooming. At summer's end, carefully replant crown divisions and keep them well watered. Foxglove also may be planted from seed sown in mid- to late summer. The 'Foxy' cultivar of *D. purpurea* seldom grows taller than 3 feet, so it is the most popular choice for containers. *D. grandiflora* is buttery yellow, reliably hardy for years in Zones 3 to 8, and petite at two to three feet tall. Its pale yellow flower spikes are a nice addition to the late spring garden. *D. purpurea* is a biennial, so it only produces leaves the first year, then blooms and dies the next.

PLANTING IDEA Use *D. grandiflora* in permanent stone containers to bring floral drama to partially shaded areas. Combine it with periwinkle vine and

add annual impatiens for color from summer to fall.

Fuchsia
Fuchsia hybrids.
Zones 7 to 11

Fuchsia is an ideal plant for hanging baskets. Arching branches with glossy green leaves are adorned with exotic looking, dangling flowers with the old

Fuchsia.

Dark pink zonal geranium.

Geranium.

Variegated geraniums, trained as standards.

Geranium foliage may be finely cut, variegated or velvety soft.

8 inches to several feet tall and wide. The main types are *P. hortorum* hybrids, the usual upright bedding plants. These geraniums are often called zonal geraniums since cool weather causes most cultivars to develop colorful zones or rings within the leaves. Many geraniums are grown as indoor-outdoor pot plants for their fancy colorful leaves and constant production of dainty flowers.

Other geranium selections include upright Martha Washington geraniums, which perform beautifully on the West Coast, ivy-leafed geraniums, which trail and are used in hanging baskets in cool summer climates and scented geraniums, which are very bushy, semi-hardy plants that bloom only sporadically but boast fragrant leaves that smell of apple, mint, chocolate or lemon. All geraniums are grown the same way. Shift plants into larger pots as soon as you buy them, and give them a rich but sandy potting soil. Put them in full sun until midsummer, and then move them to partial shade when hot weather reigns. Fertilize lightly every two weeks through the summer, but give the plants a two-month rest period in winter during which the plants should be watered very lightly. Root stem cuttings taken in late summer (to grow indoors through winter), or hold pots through winter in a cool basement or other place where they will not freeze, and take cuttings in early spring.

PLANTING IDEA The classic windowbox planting is a line of red geraniums above a trailing edging of variegated periwinkle vine. Another winning combination includes chartreuse-leafed geraniums such as 'Golden Crest' with yellow French marigolds, white sweet alyssum and forest-green duckfoot ivy.

Helianthemum, Rock Rose
Helianthemum nummularium
Zones 3 to 8

Rock rose, a semi-shrubby plant with great charm, performs well in a very sunny, well-drained position in dry soil amended with lime. It can grow up to 18 inches tall with many yellow, orange, white, pink or red flowers about an inch wide. Forms with double flowers stay open longer than singles. Cut the plants back after flowering ends. Propagate by taking cuttings in summer or growing new plants from seed. Containers make it possible for gardeners with warm, humid summers to grow this plant, but it is still a challenge.

Helianthemum grows best in dry but mild areas where temperatures stay in the 80s or below. In areas with cold winters, mulch plants with evergreen branches after freezing weather begins.

PLANTING IDEA Tuck rooted cuttings of rock rose into pockets of soil in crevices of sunny stone walls.

Hosta
Hosta species
Zones 4 to 9

Decorative, heart-shaped leaves with graceful lines and an array of colors and sizes make hosta an important

Hostas with impatiens and English ivy.

low-maintenance perennial for containers. Dwarf types are only a few inches tall, while large types may be nearly 3 feet in full leaf, with spires of bloom somewhat taller. Most types have lavender blooms but *H. sieboldiana* and its close relatives have huge white flowers with a marvelous scent. Peruse specialty catalogs to see leaf color choices that include chartreuse, blue-gray, white, yellow and many shades of green; many show surprising streaks or picotee edges. Hostas prefer shade or semishade and a loamy, water-retentive soil. Leaf color may fade if sun is too intense. They are not evergreen but leaves can be lovely as they turn golden in fall, to reappear in spring about the time that azaleas bloom. Divide hostas in early spring every few years if they become crowded or to get new plants. Use a strong, sharp knife to separate large clumps into smaller clumps with three or four pips (pointed buds) apiece. Keep the divisions very damp until new growth appears.

PLANTING IDEA Force some hostas into early leaf by bringing them into a warm, brightly lit place indoors. Move them outside as soon as the last spring frost has passed.

Lamb's-ear
Stachys byzantina
Zones 3 to 9

Lamb's-ear is grown for its fuzzy, gray-felted oval leaves, which children love to feel. Since the spiky flower spikes become ragged looking, cut them off when they appear. This mint relative is good for carpeting dry sites in full sun or partial shade, and is very easy to grow. Roots require little space, making it a good choice for mixed containers. Lamb's ear needs little care, and can adapt to any potting soil. Divide in spring or fall by transplanting basal stem cuttings. Many container gardeners keep a "mother clump" handy, in a low, broad container, so they will always have a source of little plants to add to container bouquets.

PLANTING IDEA Combine with liriope, red- or pink-flowered sedums and 'Palace Purple' heuchera in wide, bowl-shaped stone planters, using the lamb's-ear for the outer edging.

Lamb's-ear coordinates beautifully with annual dianthus and many other small flowers with dark green foliage.

Liriope, Lily Turf
Liriope species
Zones 6 to 9

Liriope's tough, grasslike dark green or variegated foliage is tidy and nearly evergreen. In summer it is punctuated by taller spikes of purple or white flowers, followed by black berries. The matted root growth makes liriope tricky to combine with other plants in long-term arrangements, but since it is so carefree and nice looking it always finds a place. Plants prefer sun or partial shade and well-drained soil of average fertility. Cut off flower spikes if they start to look messy. Remove winter-damaged leaves and divide if necessary, using the crown division method, in early spring.

PLANTING IDEA Use liriope to fill raised planters in difficult, exposed locations. Small, individual pots filled with liriope are fine textural accents to move about in the container garden.

Lychnis, Rose Campion
Lychnis coronaria
Zones 4 to 8

A downy white coating on leaves and stems is your clue that this is a sun-loving plant that tolerates dry conditions. Soil of average fertility is satisfactory for this old-fashioned favorite, but richer soil will give fuller growth. Lychnis tends to be a short-lived perennial, coming up from seeds in fall, staying in a neat rosette through the winter, and blooming the following year in early summer. Fortunately, it is easily grown from seeds. Often, you'll find volunteers in the garden if you have been growing this plant there. These can be lifted and transplanted to mixed floral planters. In full flower, lychnis is a branching plant 2 to 3 feet tall, with many 1-inch flowers of magenta or white with a pink eye. Deadhead to keep plants neat and encourage new growth.

PLANTING IDEA For a luminous display in large containers, surround rose campion with pink and white petunias laced with annual white baby's breath.

Lychnis with verbena.

Penstemon
Penstemon species
Zones 3 to 8, many types

There are many species of penstemon, many of which are native to the western United States. All have in common a penchant for gritty soil that

Penstemon.

drains very quickly, and poor tolerance of wet conditions in winter, when they are dormant. The best selections for containers grow to less than 2 feet tall. One selection, called 'Husker Red', has vibrant red foliage and produces white flowers in early summer. Grow all penstemons in sun or partial shade, and fertilize monthly. Remove faded flowers to keep the plants neat. Plants multiply quickly, forming several new plants clustered around the base. Nick these off with a sharp knife and replant them immediately in early spring. Do not let them become too crowded.

PLANTING IDEA In a large tub or planter, mix 'Husker Red' with pink, rose, white and purple flowering plants such as cosmos, baby's breath, phlox and oriental lilies. Add a few silvery touches of artemisia for striking contrast.

Phlox, creeping
Phlox subulata
Zones 3 to 8

This spring-bloomer symbolizes sweet dreams and proposals in the Victorian language of flowers. This is the low-growing, shallow-rooted phlox that covers the ground with hot pink, red,

white or blue flowers about when azaleas bloom, growing only 4 or 5 inches tall but a foot or more wide. It likes sun or partial shade and fertile, well-drained soil. After blooming, the foliage becomes a dark green mat that works well as a ground cover. Basal stem cuttings, with or without roots, will start growing within two weeks when set in moist pots filled with a sandy potting soil in fall.

PLANTING IDEA Use creeping phlox to carpet the ground beneath larger shrubs or perennials in containers. When planting daffodils or other spring-flowering bulbs in the fall, tuck a few sprigs of creeping phlox around the container's edges.

Primula
Primula species
Zones 3 to 8

There are many species and cultivars of primula, so check with local suppliers for those that are permanent and hardy in your area. Or use non-hardy greenhouse types as temporary decorative accents. Most primulas are from 6 to 12 inches tall with large clusters of small, bright flowers above oval,

Primulas.

crinkled leaves. This symbol of young love likes cool weather and is one of the first flowers of spring. Plants need rich but well-drained potting soil containing compost or organic matter and a sunny or semi-shady site. Climates with cool summers are best for growing primroses in permanent plantings. They can be grown as spring bloomers where summers are hot, and then retired to a shady spot. The 'Barnhaven' strains of polyanthus primroses are longer-lived than most others.

PLANTING IDEA In a large bulb pot, encircle a clump of red or yellow Darwin tulips with red primulas with yellow eyes. Or choose white tulips and blue and yellow primulas. Primulas are perfect for spring window boxes, though you will may need to replace them with heat tolerant annuals in early summer.

Rudbeckia
Rudbeckia species
Zones 3 to 9

The large rudbeckia family includes an assortment of perennials that grow easily from seeds. Seedlings will bloom

Bright rudbeckia.

the first year if sown indoors in late winter, or outdoors in fall through Zone 7. *Rudbeckia hirta* is our sun-loving native black-eyed Susan, 12 to 36 inches tall, with a brown center and golden ray flowers. Rudbeckias thrive in full sun, though they can take a few hours of afternoon shade in the South. If flower heads are not cut off, rudbeckias self sow in fall, and your garden may be a source of starter plants for containers. Their hairy texture helps distinguish them from weeds. Transplant them when they have four or more leaves. Most rudbeckias are not long lived, so keep a supply of new plants coming along by letting a few of the flowers go to seed. The cultivar 'Goldsturm' is more permanent than most others. It often develops rosettes of leaves near the base of the parent plant, which can be nicked off and transplanted to new pots in late summer.

PLANTING IDEA Make a sunny meadow in a half whiskey barrel. Fill it with good planting soil and then cram it with rudbeckias, daisies and coreopsis. Cosmos, poppies and other annuals can be included, too. You'll have flowers galore, and lots of bees and butterflies.

Salvia, Sage
Salvia species
Types for all zones

The huge sage genus includes many perennial species that bloom in summer or fall. The best for container gardens have many spires of blue flowers. *Salvia* 'May Night', a dwarf form only 18 to 24 inches tall, spews out a dense cover of blue spires for two months and is hardy in Zones 4 to 8. *Salvia nemerosa* has a more open form and lighter color, but is about the same size and hardiness. Purple-flowered *Salvia leucantha* gets shrub-like where it is hardy, in Zones 9 to 11. Elsewhere, plants may be pruned back in fall and held in a semi-dormant state in a cool

place through winter. Pineapple sage (*Salvia elegans*) makes a flaming red fountain about 3 feet tall. It is perennial in low-frost areas (Zones 9 to 11) but farther north it may be used as an annual. There are many other salvias, some very hardy, some tender. All types like a sunny position in well-drained, fertile potting soil. Deadhead and trim as needed. Thin and divide in early spring if plants become crowded. Stem cuttings taken in spring or fall root with relative ease.

PLANTING IDEA Combine *Salvia* 'May Night' with *Penstemon* 'Husker Red' and watch the rich blue flowers of the salvia pick up the same tones in the purple foliage of the penstemon.

Saxifrage
Saxifraga species
Types for all zones

Strawberry begonia (*Saxifraga stolonifera*) is useful as a container plant for shade in all zones. It is hardy where summers are not too hot and as far north as Zone 6, and it also thrives indoors. The nearly round, downy green leaves are touched with silver and bloom for about six weeks in

Saxifrage, or strawberry begonia.

spring with 10-inch sprays of delicate white flowers. Runners make it a willing spreader, but it is not invasive. It is especially pretty near water. Other saxifrages are diverse and include numerous species. Most are mound-forming rock garden plants preferring alpine conditions of sun, gritty alkaline soil, good drainage and cool summers.

PLANTING IDEA Use a stone or stone-like container filled with silvery strawberry begonia for a bright accent in deep shade.

Sedum
Sedum species
Zones 3 to 9, most types

Sedums and other succulents are great container plants because they hold up well in dry, sunny and windy sites but also tolerate milder, damper conditions. 'Autumn Joy' sedum is a 2-foot tall showy flower that stays in bloom for months, starting with pink blooms that age to rose, wine and finally brown. Other types are low, thick-leafed creepers that grow only a few inches tall. All sedums are tremendously versatile in containers, highly tolerant of neglect and willing to adapt to dryness or regular moisture. You can easily restrain rampant creepers like *Sedum acre* by using them as edging plants in container bouquets.

PLANTING IDEA Fill a low dish or stone trough with a mixture of soil, sand and

Showy sedum's flowers open pink and gradually change to rusty brown.

pebbles and plant it densely with a collection of sedums and other little succulents. Drainage holes are a must.

Verbena
Verbena species
Types for all zones

Garden verbenas are spreading or trailing plants with many bright

Verbena.

clusters of small, tubular flowers that are excellent for baskets, window boxes, or large pots. The color range includes terrific blues, purples, reds, coral and white. Garden verbenas are of mixed or hybrid origin and should usually be treated as annuals. They prefer full sun and rich but very well-drained soil, and regular light fertilization. Seed is fairly slow and tricky, so most gardeners buy plants. Moss verbena (*V. tenuisecta*) is easy and hardy in Zones 8 to 11 and blooms with lavender flowers. 'Homestead Purple' is a strong-growing, purple-flowered verbena that is hardy to Zone 7, but most other strains are killed by hard freezes. To hold a favorite from one year to the next, take cuttings in early fall and root them, and keep them alive in a cool window through winter.

PLANTING IDEA Spark your mixed containers with verbena in accent colors.

Vinca Minor (Myrtle), Vinca Major (Vinca Vine)
Vinca species
Hardiness varies with type.

Vinca's trailing habit and evergreen leaves make it a valuable addition to all sorts of containers. It drapes over the edges of tall pots and window boxes, and adds vertical interest to containers filled with upright plants. Vinca is hardy and easy to grow, and takes root spontaneously wherever the vines touch the soil for a few weeks. In either species, small flat-faced flowers, usually blue, appear fleetingly in spring. Vinca major, hardy to Zone 6, is deservedly popular in its variegated form, which has large leaves marked with varying shades of green and white. Window box gardeners find it indispensable. As an alternative to buying dozens of plants in spring, shear back those grown during the summer, and allow them to dry out. Hold them through winter in a cool garage or basement, watering very sparingly. Then move the containers outdoors first thing in spring, and transplant to new containers as soon as new growth appears.

Comparatively petite myrtle is usually a solid dark green but there are variegated forms. It is hardy to Zone 4, and makes a great groundcover beneath open shrubs and trees in large containers. Either type of vinca will grow well in any well-drained soil in partial sun.

PLANTING IDEA Densely fill a weatherproof trough with carefree evergreen dwarf conifers and variegated vinca vine. In summer, tuck in some red geraniums and white alyssum.

Viola, Heartsease
Viola tricolor
Zones 4 to 10

Small in flower but great in impact, the pretty viola, looking like a miniature pansy, makes bright clusters of upturned flat-faced, whiskered flowers in shades of white, purple and yellow. Flower size is under an inch, and plant height ranges from 6 to 12

Vinca minor.

inches. Violas like cool weather and are killed by high heat and humidity. Give them bright sun to bright partial shade, and rich, moist yet well-drained soil. They can be transplanted from the garden, or simply bought as bedding plants in late winter or early spring. In Zones 9 and 10, violas are grown as winter annuals, like pansies. In cool northern climates, they grow as perennials and are at their best in spring and fall.

PLANTING IDEA Line a pretty basket with a thin layer of dry sphagnum moss or other packaged moss, and then add a second lining of aluminum foil in which you have made a few drainage holes. Partially fill it with loose, rich, pre-moistened potting soil. Set in 12 to 18 viola plants, or enough to fill the basket. Fill the spaces with more potting mix, tamp down well and water. Tuck in bits of moss between the violas and water again, and place on a sunny wall or table. It will remain attractive for about eight weeks.

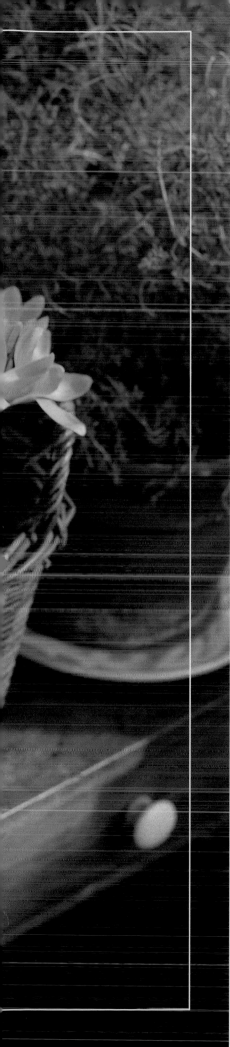

Chapter 7

❧

BULBS, CORMS RHIZOMES AND TUBERS

It is inspiring to garden with bulbs because they are easy to handle and provide refreshing colors, textures and scents. Group snowdrops, crocuses, tulips, daffodils, lilies, dahlias, hyacinths and cannas in containers for a wonderful display. Because the root systems of these plants are compact, you can set small pots of blooming bulbs into planting holes in large containers for instant results. When the flowers are past their prime, replace the pots with other bulbs or summer annuals.

Bulbs, corms, rhizomes and tubers are small, fleshy underground structures that keep certain plants alive through difficult weather. Normally, those you buy are in their dormant phase. For a good start, plant them as soon as possible after purchase. With each bulb or bulblike structure, you are getting an entire plant, ready to grow, packed by

Yellow crocuses, forced into bloom in a pot, in the happy company of a kalanchoe.

What Is A Bulb?

TRUE BULB. A true bulb, such as a tulip or daffodil, has a bud (miniature flower and leaves) surrounded and protected by thick, white scales containing enough food for bloom. These are anchored to a basal plate. A protective brown papery skin called a tunic surrounds the whole bulb, including the scales. Bulbs generally have an elongated onion shape. The uppermost tip is called the nose, which is the top of the bulb. Some bulbs are really two separate bulbs connected at the base, and are referred to as double-nosed. If the tunic is removed, the bulb will not necessarily be harmed.

CORM. A corm, such as crocus or gladiolus, is similar to a bulb, but most of the food is stored in the basal plate rather than in the scales, which are much smaller than those in bulbs. Corms generally have a round but flattened shape. A tunic (sometimes composed of several layers) surrounds the corm.

RHIZOME. A rhizome is a thickened piece of root-like stem. It grows horizontally underground or at the surface of the soil. Plants emerge from buds at the ends. Bearded iris and canna lilies are good examples.

TUBER. A tuber is a thickened root-like piece of stem tissue that does not have a removable tunic, but does have at least one bud or eye. Dahlias, sweet potatoes, white potatoes and tuberous begonias are tubers. Shapes vary from round and smooth to pointy or lumpy and irregular. Some, like dahlias, grow in complex clusters.

---

nature inside a tidy package. Plants from these structures can also be purchased already growing or even blooming in pots, or they can be transplanted from the garden either as growing plants or during their dormant phase. There are frost-hardy types, which usually bloom in spring, and frost-tender types, which usually bloom in summer.

WAYS TO USE BULBS IN CONTAINERS

Whether for short-term accents or long-term displays, bulbs make great container plants. You can use any kind if you give it the appropriate container and growing conditions. Use bulbs in combination with other plants or use masses of the same type in a single container. In most cases, dwarf and low-growing types are best because they need no staking. Combination plantings are more successful if all types bloom at the same time for a really big show. Attractive foliage and everblooming plants extend the decorative period.

If you have permanent outdoor planters and large containers, plant bulbs in them as if you were planting them in a garden. You may remove them after they bloom, because you will not want to see the lingering foliage. Early bloomers with inconspicuous foliage, such as snowdrops and crocus, are very effective planted in weatherproof containers near entranceways and paths. During warm weather, begonias, cannas, caladiums and dahlias provide color for months.

POTTING AND FORCING HARDY BULBS THAT NEED CHILLING

Most of our familiar spring-blooming bulbs are hybrids of hardy plants that grow wild in the Mediterranean and Middle East. In these regions with hot, dry summers, bulbs store leaves and flowers in miniature in thickened, often waxy underground structures, along with food for the emerging plant. This is the bulb that we plant in the fall. With the arrival of cool, wet weather, hardy bulbs take a cue from nature and start to grow roots. In spring they rapidly sprout leaves and shoot up stalks of flowers for brief but spectacular bloom, just once a year. We "force" bulbs by manipulating moisture, light and temperature to change the bloom time or help the bulbs bloom in warm climates. Most spring-blooming bulbs require chilling in winter.

Whether or not you want to force the bulbs into early bloom, you can pot them up the same way. Use clean potting mix to prevent pests and diseases. A good formula is one third each of peat moss, loamy soil and coarse sand. Plant bulbs in either plastic pots or the pots in which you intend to show the flowers. Bulb pans about 6 inches deep and 10 inches wide are great. Plant large bulbs such as tulips and daffodils in two staggered layers to pack more flowers into the pot. Be sure to label containers because they look alike.

Hobbyists forcing hardy bulbs for bloom on a certain date, such as for a flower show, have quite a challenge, and usually have several backup containers. If they vary the chilling and growing time, they'll get at least one just right. But simply forcing bulbs to be a little early is not at all difficult. Plant up and water the containers in October to start root development. Choose early-blooming types for best results: early rather than late-blooming tulips, for instance.

If you live in a hot climate, keep the planted pots in a refrigerator for 10 to 14 weeks, checking to make sure that the soil stays barely moist. If the bulbs start to sprout, bring them out and grow them in a brightly lit place, but not too hot a spot or it will make them leggy. Keep the temperature under 60°F at night. If the bulbs don't show sprouts, bring them into well-lighted conditions at the end of the chilling period. You might also check at your nursery, for they may sell pre-chilled, pre-conditioned bulbs that are ready to plant.

If you live in a climate with cold winters, you can treat the bulbs the same way just described, or you can use outdoor weather to help you force or grow them. Pot up, label and water the bulbs. Set them in an out-of-the-way place such as a side yard, covered with mesh or screening to keep out squirrels. As weather gets colder with more frosty nights, move them into a coldframe or covered window well, or else cover sides and tops with a 2-foot layer of chopped leaves or wood chips. Leave them there for at least 10 weeks. Then bring them into warmer, brighter conditions. You can vary the timing of this, but be on the lookout for pots that are starting to sprout on their own. They should come in first. Bring them into the spotlight as they come nearer to bloom. Give them plenty of light. Long artificial day length, such as 16 hours of bright light and cool temperatures, keep stems short.

If you cannot provide the right indoor conditions, grow the pots of bulbs outside naturally. Uncover pots that are mulched after snow starts to melt and sprouts start to show in the pots or in neighboring gardens.

After bloom, leaves and roots continue gathering energy until they have rebuilt a strong bulb for next year's plant. Be sure to fertilize them after the blooms are gone. If times are good, bulbs will multiply by dividing into several smaller bulbs. Seeds may form from the flower if permitted, but in most cases it is better to pinch them off. This causes the plants to channel their energy toward rebuilding the bulb. When grown in containers, bulbs are sometimes disposed of after flowering, but in many cases they can be treated to deluxe conditions and given a second chance.

GROWING TENDER BULBS AND TUBERS

Summer-blooming bulbs, corms, rhizomes and tubers such as dahlia, lily, anemone, canna and tuberous begonia come from diverse regions and climates, but they grow in similar ways to spring-flowering bulbs. Except for lilies, they tend to be frost-tender. In colder regions such as Zones 3 to 8 they are planted outdoors after frost

in late spring, but in warmer regions they may be planted in winter or left out all year. In frost-free or low-frost zones, so-called summer bloomers such as amaryllis and gladiolus may flower in cool months such as February and March.

Paperwhite narcissus are favorite bulbs for forcing into bloom in containers. Start them in fall or winter.

In areas with cold winters, store non-hardy bulbous plants in a cool place indoors until after the danger of frost passes. If you have a cool basement or garage where winter temperatures will not fall below around 30°F, you can leave many summer-flowering bulbs and tubers in their containers, and allow them to dry out and become dormant right in their pots. In spring, repot the roots by shifting them to slightly larger containers, and give them water and light to coax them out of dormancy. This easy method works quite well with amaryllis, canna, iris and sweet potato.

Some thick-rooted flowers are prone to so many types of root rot that it is better to remove them from containers, rinse them clean and allow them to cure in a dry place before storing them for winter. Tuberous begonias, caladiums and dahlias are best handled this way. You can pack them in small boxes filled with perlite or sand, or simply place them in a cool place lightly covered with sterile soilless potting mix. Check the roots from time to time during the winter to make sure they are not drying out too much. In very dry interior places, it is helpful to sprinkle stored roots with water about once a month.

A Gallery of Bulbs, Corms, Rhizomes and Tubers

Among 23 versatile selections, you will find flowering bulbs and tubers for every season and climate.

Aconite, Winter
Eranthis hyemalis
Zones 5 to 8

This yellow flower, related to buttercups, is about an inch wide on four-inch-tall stems. Blooms are so early that they often pop up through a frosting of snow. Plant tubers an inch deep in rich, moist but well-drained soil. Place the planted containers in sun or under deciduous trees that are bare in winter. The tubers dry out quickly in storage, so buy them early in fall, checking to make sure they are still plump. Winter aconite is a good companion to other spring bulbs that bloom a little later. The star-shaped seedpods and low-growing divided foliage are attractive as they ripen from green to tan.

PLANTING IDEA In fall, plant a low stone bowl with sprigs of small-leafed ivy, winter aconite, snowdrops and 'Barrett Browning', an early dwarf white narcissus with red-orange cups. When the aconites sprout, place the pot near a doorway.

Allium
Allium species
Hardiness varies with type

Alliums are ornamental onions with flowers in rounded clusters. Alliums combine well with other bulbs and flowers planted in fall, for they do not need much root space. They like sun and rich, well-drained but moist soil. Most types are hardy as far north as Zone 4. Ornamental alliums range from a few inches to over 4 feet in height, so match your choice to the container's size and contents. Shorter-stemmed alliums that are especially good for containers include *Allium moly*, a yellow flower grown as a talisman for good luck; *A. neapoli-*

tanum, a pretty white-flowered selection; petite rose-pink *A. oreophilum* and *A. karataviense*, a very broad-leafed allium with huge silvery flowers on 6-inch stems.

PLANTING IDEA Combine striking *A. karataviense* with everblooming white violas or white sweet alyssum.

Amaryllis
Hippeastrum hybrids
All Zones, with protection, Hardy in Zones 9 to 11

Amaryllis is one of the easiest and most rewarding bulbs to grow in containers. The huge trumpet-like flowers are up to eight inches across, with up to four flowers per stalk. Leaves are glossy, broad and strap-like. Flower color may be red, white, pink, peach or magenta. Prepotted, preconditioned bulbs are widely available in 6-inch pots, but any amaryllis bulbs are easy to force indoors in winter, in rich, moist, well-drained, slightly acidic potting soil. With a minimum of care, they will rebloom for many years.

To plant, place a single large bulb in a container only 2 inches wider than the diameter of the bulb, and allow the top of the bulb to show above the soil. Water enough to keep the soil lightly moist until the first leaf bud appears. Then move the pot to good light (such as a south-facing windowsill), and

Amaryllis.

water as needed to keep the soil constantly moist. Blooms will appear about six weeks after the first leaves emerge. For blooms at Christmas, plant amaryllis bulbs indoors in the middle of October.

When the blooms start to fade, remove the stalk and flowers but let the leaves continue to grow. Fertilize about once a month. When the danger of frost passes, set the plants outside for the summer in bright partial shade. Stop fertilizing and watering at the end of summer. When the foliage yellows and frost is imminent, snip off the leaves and bring the plants into a cool, dry place. The bulbs need a rest period of about six weeks, but can remain dormant for up to three months in dry pots. Bring them back to life by repotting (if desired), and providing water and warmth. Amaryllis, native to South Africa, is perfectly hardy outdoors in low-frost zones.

PLANTING IDEA Three amaryllis bulbs blooming in an attractive container make a perfect holiday gift for any gardener. The 'Scarlet Baby' cultivar is a fine choice for beginners.

Anemone, Windflower
Anemone blanda, A. coronaria
Zones vary with species

Also called Grecian windflower, *Anemone blanda* is hardy to Zone 5 and blooms at about the same time as tulips. Plant tubers in fall, 4 to 5 inches deep and 2 or more inches apart, in a sunny exposure. In spring you will have many 6-inch plants with delicate, daisylike flowers in white, pink and blue, with yellow centers. This flower needs little space. It makes a nice accent in its own container or underplanted with other plants. Protect tubers from rodents.

Less winter hardy but equally easy to grow, poppy anemones (*A. coronaria*) are popular for pots and cut flowers. Hardy to Zone 6, the vivid blossoms may be pink, red, white or blue with

Anemones.

black centers. Foliage is finely divided and attractive. Poppy anemones prefer bright partial shade but can also be grown in full sun if the climate is not too hot. For best results, soak the flat black rhizomes in water for several hours before planting, but no longer than overnight. Plant about 4 inches deep and 8 inches apart in rich, well-drained soil with a neutral pH. Try a fall planting in mild climates. In Zones 5 to 7, set the pot in a coldframe or cool greenhouse in winter, and move it outdoors at about the time of the last expected frost.

PLANTING IDEA Combine *Anemone coronaria* with white sweet alyssum and trailing periwinkle vine.

Basket Flower, Peruvian Daffodil, Ismene

Hymenocallis narcissiflora and other species
All Zones, with protection Hardy in Zones 9 to 11

Basket flowers, with 4-inch yellow or white flowers that resemble spidery-petaled daffodils with green eyes, are 2 feet tall in bloom. Straplike leaves are deep green and about 2 inches wide.

There are quite a few *Hymenocallis* species, all of which are bulbous plants related to amaryllis. They prefer moist, rich soil and should be protected from frost. Basket flowers make good substitutes for daffodils in warm, frost-free climates and bloom year after year. Propagate new plants from seeds or offsets.

PLANTING IDEA Use basket-flowers indoors or out in a decorative container. In the South, make a permanent outdoor display of them.

Begonia, Tuberous

Begonia hybrids.
All Zones, with protection, hardy in Zones 9 to 11

Tuberous begonias are succulent plants that can be used indoors or outdoors in partial shade. They are among the most colorful container plants for shady places. Those from tubers have decorative leaves in an asymmetric paisley shape, and brilliantly colored waxy flowers of varied sizes. Flower color may be white, yellow, pink, orange or red, and foliage may be green or bronze. Start begonias from packaged tubers in a frost-free place in spring, or purchase plants already growing in pots or hanging baskets. In areas with cold winters, allow the plants to dry completely in fall, and store the tubers in a frost-free place until time to restart them indoors in early spring. Begonias grow best in

Tuberous begonias.

rich, well-drained, slightly acid soil. Provide a semi-shady site and constant moisture. Protect them from slugs. Keep your plants in glowing form with frequent light feedings.

PLANTING IDEA Combine shade-loving begonias with ivy, fuchsia or nicotiana.

Caladium
Caladium hybrids
All Zones with protection, hardy in
    Zones 9 to 11

Caladiums are grown for their brightly variegated heart-shaped leaves rather than their flowers. The color range includes white, yellow, red, pink and several shades of green. Some combinations can be very gaudy. Caladiums are especially useful in shady spots in warm, humid climates. Start tubers in late spring or summer, planting them about 3 inches deep. They prefer moist, rich, well-drained soil. Set the pots outdoors after soil is warm. Dig and store the tubers in fall, before frost, in a dry, cool place.

PLANTING IDEA Brighten a shady spot by making a white garden in a low, wide container. Use white-flowered impatiens and tuberous begonias with green- and white-leafed caladiums.

Canna
Canna hybrids
All Zones, with protection, hardy in
    Zones 7 to 11

Here is a Victorian plant that is coming back into style. Cannas have broad, tropical looking leaves that are highly effective when grown in large tubs and containers. The best cannas for containers are dwarf types that grow to about three feet tall. Cannas thrive in moist, hot weather, and some will grow as emergent plants in water gardens. Plant them in full sun or bright partial shade and provide plenty of water and fertilizer. To plant, lay dormant rhizomes on their sides and cover with 2 inches of soil. The larger the pots, the faster and better cannas will grow. Divide cannas when they become so crowded that they need water more than once a day. Some of the best cannas have colored foliage, which may be purple, bronze or green variegated with yellow or white stripes. Flowers may be cream, yellow, orange, red or pink. In cold winter areas, let the plants dry off for a few days and bring the container indoors in fall. Cut back foliage and store in a dry, cool but frost-free area. Or, dig up the rhizomes and store them in barely moistened peat moss inside ventilated plastic bags.

PLANTING IDEA Combine purple-leafed, pink-flowering cannas with pink, green and white caladiums and pink and green-leafed coleus with lacy edges.

Crocus
Crocus species and hybrids
Zones 3 to 8

The key with crocus is quantity. First thing in spring, it is delightful to have many small cuplike flowers in white, yellow, orange, pink and purple peeking out of the soil. The hardy corms are widely available, inexpensive and easy to force. Crocus prefers well-drained soil and lots of sun. Spring-blooming species such as the lavender-flowered snow crocus are smaller and earlier than hybrids. All crocuses have narrow grass-like foliage which lingers but is much less conspicuous than that of daffodils. In cold-winter areas, closely plant corms about 3 inches deep in small pots in September or October. You can fit as many as 15 in a 4-inch pot if you stagger them in two layers. To force them, grow them in a cold-frame or refrigerator for 10 to 12 weeks and then bring them inside. Or plant in weatherproof planters outdoors for bloom at the normal time. Several

Caladiums.

Bright yellow crocuses.

types including the saffron crocus bloom in fall. Dig and respace corms every few years if they are crowded. Protect from rabbits, squirrels and other animals.

PLANTING IDEA Force several small pots of crocus and replant them in baskets for tabletop decorations in late winter.

Daffodils, Narcissus
Narcissus species and hybrids
Zones 3 to 8, most types

Daffodils are among the most reliable of bulbs. They like any well-drained soil and full sun or partial shade. They have built-in pest-proofing because they are toxic if eaten. There are hundreds of named types currently available that grow from a few inches to nearly 2 feet tall. They may be single or multiple flowered, with short, long, split or frilled cups. The whites and yellows are best known, but cups may also be red-orange or pink. Jonquilla types are fragrant and heat tolerant, good for southern gardens. Short-stemmed types such as 'February Gold' are neat in containers for they require no staking. Early-blooming types are best for forcing, for they need less pre-chilling. Fill pots with two layers of bulbs for fuller pots. Keep soil slightly moist but not soggy. After flowering, let plants grow and fertilize regularly for about six weeks until they turn yellow, if you want bulbs to rebloom.

Dainty narcissus.

Chilling is not required for paperwhites (*N. tazetta*), which are the best kind of daffodil to force into bloom indoors. Buy the bulbs in fall and plant in bowls about 3 inches deep. Use small stones or a soilless potting mix, and grow them in a brightly lit place. With so many small flowers per stem, they tend to be top heavy. Stake them by encircling the group of stalks with strings and bamboo skewers or small sticks, but do not puncture bulbs or roots. Paperwhites are hardy outdoors in Zones 9 and 10, but normally do not flower again after forcing.

PLANTING IDEA Combine daffodils with perennials whose foliage appears late in spring, such as ferns or hosta. This covers up the fading daffodil leaves. In summer, use annuals to brighten pots where dormant daffodils are at rest.

Dahlia
Dahlia hybrids
All Zones with protection, hardy in
Zones 8 to 10

Dahlias grow into bushy, branching plants with many colorful flowers. As with zinnias, there is great variety in size and flower form. Dahlias bloom in all colors but blue. Dwarf dahlias with low bushy foliage and a profusion of 2- to 3-inch flowers are easiest to use in pots and window boxes. Plant the dormant roots in pots in early spring, and place them outdoors after the danger of frost passes. Pinch the tips off shoots when they are a few inches tall to promote side branching. Dahlias reflower for many weeks from summer to fall. They like sun, rich, moist soil and regular fertilization. In hot weather, pots

Dahlias preside over a mass of annuals.

A Gallery of Bulbs, Corms, Rhizomes and Tubers

and stems and a checkered bell-shaped flower. It is usually purple and white, but a white-on-white form is also available. Soil needs are similar. Plant bulbs 4 inches deep.

PLANTING IDEA In half a whiskey or wine barrel, plant six crown imperials with pansies and variegated ivy.

Glory of the Snow
Chionodoxa species
Zones 4 to 8

A periwinkle-blue flower that will always draw compliments is glory of the snow. Large numbers of the blue-flowered types create the impression of a misty blue haze. There is also a pink form that blooms in early spring with delicate clusters of white centered blossoms on 6-inch stems. In fall, plant bulbs 3 inches deep in any good, well-drained soil, and set pots in partial shade or under deciduous trees. With their small, shallow bulbs and harmonious colors, chionodoxas are good companions in mixed planters.

PLANTING IDEA In fall, fill a tiny stone trough with white crocus and blue glory of the snow, planting densely and topping with moss or grass. Enjoy the sight in spring.

Grape Hyacinth
Muscari species.
Zones 4 to 8

Grape hyacinths give you a good way to add bright, strong blue to your containers. The bulbs produce spikes of small round flowers that look like tiny clusters of grapes. There is also a white form that has been called pearls of Spain. All grape hyacinths are effective planted under shrubs in broad containers. Plant them 4 inches deep and provide rich, well-drained soil and partial to full sun. The long, narrow leaves last for months and must be left on the plants to ripen if you want the plants to rebloom.

may need watering more than once a day. From Zone 7 northward, store tubers in a frost-free place in winter, but keep them from drying or rotting. Pack them in slightly moistened peat moss or perlite in plastic bags with ventilation holes, or close them in paper grocery sacks with some of their soil still clinging to the tubers. In either case, cut off tops and expose tubers to sun for a few days before storing them in a cool basement room (50 to 60°F) until early spring. Repot and grow indoors until warm weather and safe planting time return.

PLANTING IDEA Fill a windowbox with perky 'Collarette' dwarf dahlias.

Fritillary, Crown Imperial, Guinea Flower
Fritillaria species
Zones 4 to 8

Crown Imperial, (*Fritillaria imperialis*) may be the showiest flower in the spring garden. It can grow 4 feet tall with a broad cluster of bell-shaped yellow, orange or red flowers suspended from a stout stalk. Plant it in fall, 8 inches deep, in roomy pots filled with moist, free-draining soil. Plant three or more bulbs together for a better looking arrangement. Guinea flower (*Fritillaria meleagris*) is much smaller, under a foot tall, with narrow leaves

Grape hyacinth.

Hyacinths.

Unlike most other spring-flowering bulbs, grape hyacinths produce new leaves in autumn, which persist all winter. They are not good bulbs for forcing.

PLANTING IDEA Combine grape hyacinths with lacy white perennial candytuft, all colors of primulas and red tulips.

Hyacinth
Hyacinthus orientalis
Zones 4 to 8

Great colors, a bold form and sweet scent make these a container garden favorite. Hyacinth flowers are densely filled spikes studded with colorful florets that may be white, pink, red, violet, pale yellow and many shades of blue. For spring bloom, plant them in fall and place the pots in sun or partial shade through winter. The large bulbs can be grown in small containers or crowded into larger ones only 1 inch apart, for the bulb provides most of the food needed to support strong blooming. Hyacinths are very easy to force into bloom indoors in winter following a period of chilling. For this use, plant bulbs in fall and place the planted pot outdoors in a protected place for about a month. In mild climates, simply place the bulbs in your refrigerator for a month before

planting them. After a month of damp cold, bring the pots into a cool, dark place for about two weeks. After the first green shoots emerge from the tops of the bulbs, move the pots to strong light and keep the soil constantly moist. Flowers should appear a few weeks later. After forcing, allow the foliage to ripen to build strength for the next year's flowers. Even when given very good care, hyacinths tend to lose vigor after the first year or two.

PLANTING IDEA In spring, buy hyacinths in bloom in individual small pots. Use them in a combination planting with pansies, primulas and evergreen filler such as ivy, making holes for the hyacinth pots. Later, replace them with dwarf dahlias.

Iris
Iris species and hybrids
Types for all Zones

There are about 200 species of iris, but some of them are much better for containers than others. The bulbous *Iris reticulata* (all colors) and *Iris danfordiae* (yellow) are only a few inches tall. They are hardy in Zones 3 to 9, bloom early, and are easy to force. Treat them like crocus, and move the pots to an out-of-the-way place after the flowers fade, for the long leaves tend to flop over and are not particu-

larly attractive. Dutch, English and Spanish irises bloom in mid-spring and early summer, in a rainbow of colors on 18-inch stems. They, too, are bulbous, but not quite as hardy, growing as perennials mainly in Zones 6 to 8. Other irises may have bulbous, fibrous or rhizomatous roots. Siberian (*I. siberica*) and Japanese iris (*I. ensata*) are useful in containers where you want a strongly upright element. Their sword-shaped leaves stay crisp and neat. Blooms are magnificent for a brief period in spring. Beautiful bearded irises (*I. germanica*, Zones 4 to 8) are somewhat tricky to use in containers because of their bulky size. All irises thrive in full sun to bright partial shade. Grow them in moist but well-drained soil of average fertility. Siberian and Japanese irises also grow well in damp or wet soil.

PLANTING IDEA Buy a good supply of inexpensive *I. reticulata* in your favorite colors and force them by the potful. Every few days, bring another pot out of cooler storage for a succession of bloom.

Lily
Lilium hybrids
Zones 4 to 9

Elegance is the hallmark of the lily. A large 24-inch pot will house a half dozen large lilies or a dozen dwarf ones for a fantastic show. Lilies prefer well-drained soil in sun or partial shade. They are suited to pot culture, and the pots help protect them from pests. Plant lily bulbs about 6 inches deep in frostproof containers in fall or early spring. Heap mulch around and over the pots you plant up in fall. If squirrels are numerous in your area, cover the pots with polyester netting or window screening to protect the bulbs from these little gnawing thieves. Remove the mulch in spring, about when early daffodils bloom. You can bring fall-planted pots into warm, bright areas indoors to force the lilies

Asiatic lilies.

flowers. After blooms finish, cut down the flower stalks but allow the foliage to ripen until it flops over.

Puschkinia
Puschkinia species
Zones 5 to 8

Commonly known as striped squills, puschkinias produce clusters of starry striped blue to white flowers on 4- to 6-inch stalks. The paired leaves are grasslike. Bulbs are inexpensive, multiply prolifically, bloom early and have few problems or pests. Plant them 3 inches deep in fall, in any good, well-drained soil. They do well in partial shade to full sun. As with other small bulbs, puschkinias combine well with other plants because they require so little space.

PLANTING IDEA In fall, pot up a planter with yellow daffodils and blue puschkinias. In spring, set it near the front door.

Scilla, Squill
Scilla species
Zones 4 to 8

Scilla grows from bulbs and closely resembles puschkinia in needs and appearance. Each bulb sprouts several four-inch spikes, with several blue or white flowers on each. *Scilla siberica* can be a strong medium blue, and there is also a pure white form. All the scillas are exceptionally easy to grow and are among the most shade-tolerant of bulbs. Plant the large bulbs 3 inches deep in shallow pots in fall or early winter. They do well in average soil with good drainage and either a sunny or partially shaded site. You can also force scillas into bloom early by bringing fall-planted pots indoors after the buds emerge in late winter.

PLANTING IDEA Enjoy the rich blue of *Scilla siberica* in midwinter by forcing it in small containers.

into early bloom, or leave them outside to bloom at the natural time. In most areas, Asiatic and tiger lilies bloom in early summer, followed by regale and Oriental lilies a few weeks later. If your container garden is shady, try martagon and turk's cap lilies, which need less sun than other types.

PLANTING IDEA When lily foliage emerges from pot-grown bulbs, add a few cascading annuals such as lobelia to conceal the lilies' bare lower stems.

Gladiolus, Peacock Orchid, Acidanthera
Gladiolus hybrids, *Gladiolus callianthus*
  (formerly *Acidanthera bicolor*)
All Zones, with protection, hardy in
  Zones 8 to 11

Gladiolus blooms aligned on tall stems are lovely but fleeting. The handsome swordlike foliage fits well into container arrangements. Five-foot garden glads are too lanky for most containers, but hardy glads (*Gladiolus communis byzantinus*) make wonderful additions to the container garden. Hardy to Zone 6, these showy 2-foot flowers may need staking to keep them upright. A container garden treasure formerly classified as *Acidanthera bicolor*, *G. callianthus* or peacock orchid, is hardy only to Zone 7. However, its fragrant white flowers blotched with dark purple make it worth the trouble of storing the pots through winter in a cool place where they will not freeze. All gladioli require full sun, well-drained soil and monthly fertilization during the summer. Corms are inexpensive so buy new ones for containers each year, perhaps using leftovers from the last year in a cutting garden.

PLANTING IDEA Spike mixed sunny containers with acidanthera for a linear foliage accent and super stems of white

Snowdrop
Galanthus species
Zones 3 to 8

The charming little white snowdrop (*Galanthus nivalis*) lives up to its name and blooms early in the year despite frost and light snow. Plants are only 4 or 5 inches tall and have nodding flowers with green tips on the petals. There is a double-flowered form that is similar in other ways, *Galanthus nivalis* 'Flore Pleno'. The giant snow-drop, *Galanthus elwesii*, is a little later to bloom, and much larger at 10 inches. All the snowdrops should be planted in early fall because the bulbs dry out easily. They are easy to force; treat them like crocus. Plant them in moist soil in partial to full shade, especially under deciduous trees.

PLANTING IDEA Plant lots of snowdrops in broad containers where they can spread, or let them grow into colonies in the ground. In late winter, dig up small clumps with a trowel when the white buds start to show. Plant them in little teacups or baskets, topping the soil with moss, for gemlike natural arrangements.

Sweet Potato
Ipomoea batatas
Grows in all zones with protection, hardy in Zones 8 to 11

Is it ornamental or is it practical? The sweet potato, which is related to morning glories, has variously shaped leaves. A popular cultivar for containers is called 'Blackie' and has strongly pointed reddish maroon leaves. All sweet potatoes develop handsome spreading vines that are excellent for hot areas. Grow slips or sprouts any time of year indoors by placing a tuber in water in a warm place, with its sprouting end facing up. When stems are more then 6 inches long, cut them off and plant them in pots of moist potting soil. In late spring, 'Blackie' and other highly ornamental cultivars are widely available in four-inch pots at retail nurseries. Green-leafed types of sweet potato look nice, but the distinctive purple-leafed form looks even better. Since the tender new growing tips of sweet potato leaves are edible, use them freely as garnishes for platters of food.

PLANTING IDEA In a large, deep container, grow trailing purple-leafed sweet potato vine with pink lilies, spiky New Zealand flax and red and purple-leafed coleus.

Tulip
Tulipa hybrids
Zones 4 to 8

The tulip, once worth the proverbial King's ransom, is now one of the best known and loved of all bulbs. The color range of the flowers includes all shades but true blue. Height and flower shape and size are amazingly varied. Shop the specialty catalogs or a good nursery for interesting choices.

For outdoor container plantings you can use any garden tulip that you like. Parrot tulips, with their streaked and highly ruffled petals, are perhaps the most fanciful and striking. Dainty species tulips are also interesting, and they are above average in their ability to become perennial in the container garden.

Tulips prefer well-drained neutral or slightly alkaline potting mixture, and full sun for the strongest stems. Make the soil rich with compost and fertilizer if you want bulbs to bloom more than once. However, it is no crime to discard tulips after bloom because new bulbs always bloom better than old ones, especially when grown in containers.

To force tulips in containers, look for types that are short-stemmed and relatively early to flower. Plant them in fall, in a double layer for more blooms per pot. You can also plant individual bulbs in 4-inch plastic pots, and transplant them to larger containers when you get ready to move them indoors. For the first month after planting, keep forcing tulips outdoors, covered with 6 inches of pine needles or other mulch. During this time, the large bulbs develop roots but no leaves. To get them to bloom very early, simply clean the pots and bring them indoors as soon as the first leaf buds emerge from the bulbs. If handled carefully, bulbs forced in small pots can be transplanted to pretty containers and will continue to grow steadily until they flower.

PLANTING IDEA Plant a weatherproof tub with Darwin tulips in coordinated shades of rose, pink, wine and white, using 12 of each, combined with a dozen dainty narcissus.

Red tulips.

Chapter 8

A COLLECTION OF HERBS

*H*erbs are perfect for containers. Container herb gardens allow any gardener with only a little time and space to enjoy the incomparable flavor of fresh basil, the invigorating fragrance of mint and the frilly beauty of parsley picked within steps of the kitchen door. Even if you have space to spare, some herbs are best grown in containers. Invasive ones that spread everywhere, such as mint, oregano and some types of thyme are best restrained by pots. Others that require exacting conditions, such as lavender, often do better in containers than in the ground.

Container herb gardens are easy to assemble and maintain on a patio or terrace, or inside a sunny window indoors. Large clay bowls and strawberry jars will hold six to nine plants for compact all-in-one gardens. A collection of various-sized pots, each filled

All the most popular culinary herbs are easy to grow in pots, including parsely, oregano, thyme, basil, rosemary and sage.

Protected in winter, rosemary can live for many years.

HARVESTING AND WINTER CARE

Just before herbs flower and during the flowering period are the best times to harvest most herbs for maximum flavor and fragrance. There are more of the aromatic oils that give herbs their flavor in needles, leaves and flowers then. Remove no more than one third of plant growth when harvesting. Regular snipping of leaves and stems actually helps many herbs by forcing the plants to branch and become bushy. Herb seeds that are used for culinary purposes such as dill and cilantro (the seeds are known as coriander) are mature when they fall to the ground. Tie a paper bag over seed heads to catch them.

Many herbs can be taken indoors when winter approaches, though they do not grow as well indoors as out. About three weeks before your first frost, cut back all plant growth by half, and clip off weak stems and runners. Scrub the outside of pots with a stiff brush dipped in a light bleach solution (one tablespoon household bleach to a quart of warm water) to remove dirt, moss and other debris. Before bringing the pots indoors, some gardeners like to drench the soil in containers with a weak insecticide solution to rid plants of any pests they may harbor. Pouring water into a pot until it drains out the bottom in a steady stream for two minutes also will dislodge pests. Salts that build up in the soil from fertilizer and tap water will be flushed away, too. When you bring your herbs indoors, place them in west or south facing windows. An inexpensive fluorescent light fixture mounted at the top of a window frame can turn a dim window into an ideal spot, too.

Hardy perennial herbs that are not brought indoors must be given some extra protection in cold-winter areas, for thin-walled pots and tubs do not insulate roots from freeze damage. Set the containers in a trench dug in the ground and cover them with a 12-inch blanket of organic mulch such as leaves, store them in cold frames or keep them in a cool basement or garage until spring.

with a different herb, makes a versatile herb garden. Grow your herbs as close to your kitchen as possible so you can gather up sprigs of parsley or basil quickly, while you are cooking. If space is really tight, try growing your favorite herbs in a hanging basket just outside the kitchen door.

Herbs also combine well with flowers and vegetables for container bouquets. A clump of garlic chives paired with a colorful lavender bell pepper and trailing yellow lantana (which is poisonous) makes a useful and decorative display for any deck or patio. Creeping thymes make aromatic edging plants for container bouquets, small trees and shrubs.

GETTING STARTED WITH HERBS

Nurseries and garden centers carry a good selection of herb plants in the spring. In addition, by asking around, you often can find local herb growers who sell plants in spring. It is always a good idea to buy perennial herbs as plants, for some grow so slowly that it takes months or even a year for seedlings to reach transplanting size. Also, some perennial herbs do not grow true from seed and are best propagated by rooting stem cuttings. Fast-growing annual herbs such as basil and dill are easy to raise from seed, but you will save time by purchasing slow-to-grow parsley as plants. Cilantro and dill are best seeded directly into containers, because they both have long tap roots and resent being transplanted.

Any potting soil will do for herbs. They are not at all fussy, except when it comes to water. Their roots like to be slightly dry, and never waterlogged. Choose a potting mix that drains well, or add a bit of sand to peaty potting soils. At the same time, herbs should not be allowed to get so dry that the plants wilt, so check their containers daily in hot weather and water as needed to keep them slightly moist.

Keep your herbs in full sun in spring and fall, and through the summer in cool climates. In warm climates, morning sun and some afternoon shade is preferable during summer months. Mint will even tolerate shade all day.

A Gallery of Container Herbs

Basil
Ocimum basilicum
Tender Annual

The most widely planted herb in gardens today, basil comes in over 150 varieties. Large-leafed ones like 'Lettuce Leaf' are big enough to wrap around fish and chicken pieces for grilling, though many gourmet cooks prefer small-leafed varieties such as 'Picolo'. Scented basils such as 'Cinnamon' and 'Lemon' basil fill the air with perfume when the plants are lightly brushed with a hand. 'Siam Queen' is a large plant that is especially attractive in midsummer, when its 3-inch purple blossom spikes cover the plants. For color contrast, pick purple-leafed basils like 'Red Rubin'. A special variety for eating and landscaping called 'Spicy Globe' grows into a neat mound of small, flavor-packed leaves. This list is just the beginning of the many basils that are available to anyone willing to plant the seeds.

Containers for basil should be eight to 12 inches wide and 10 inches deep. Two or three transplants will be happy in a 12-inch pot. This herb grows best in warm sun when temperatures range between 70 and 90°F. A heat lover, basil will not thrive unless planted or transplanted outdoors when days are at least 70°F and nights are above 55°F. Seeds can be started in a warm place indoors six weeks before the last frost date.

After potting, keep soil evenly moist, and fertilize every two weeks during the growing season. When plants reach 6 inches tall, begin harvesting by pinching out growing tips, two or three at a time. Also pinch off flower buds as soon as they appear unless you intend to use them to make basil-flavored vinegar, which tastes best when made with both flowers and leaves. Sow a second crop in midsummer for indoor use. When temperatures at night fall into the upper 50s, take potted basils indoors.

TIPS Lemon-scented basils have a refreshing flavor. Any basil makes a good companion plant for cucumbers and tomatoes in containers.

Bay
Laurus nobilis
Tender Perennial

Hardy to 28°F, container-planted bay trees must be protected in winter. Purchased seedlings can be started in

Bay.

8-inch pots and gradually moved up to tubs that can be brought indoors during freezing weather. Do not cut back bay trees before bringing them inside. Instead, do only a light tip pruning to force branching. Bay grows best in full sun, but it will tolerate light afternoon shade. Maintain moist soil and fertilize every two weeks in summer and monthly in winter. By nature, bay trees grow very slowly and are best thought of as narrow upright shrubs. (California bay laurel, *Umbellularia californica*, is a different plant that's poisonous.)

TIPS Maximize container gardening space by underplanting bay trees with trailing herbs such as thyme and marjoram. To maintain vigor, harvest sparingly until trees are two years old.

Chervil
Anthriscus cerefolium
Hardy Annual

A culinary herb with plenty of flavor punch, chervil tastes like parsley with a

Red, green, and bicolored basils.

heavy licorice overtone. Plant seeds directly into pots in spring, after the last frost has passed, or indoors three weeks before the last frost date. Set purchased transplants in 6-inch or larger pots. This feathery herb prefers cool weather and light shade, and does poorly in hot, dry conditions. It should be protected from summer sun. Keep soil evenly moist and fertilize every two weeks. For dense foliage, cut flower stems before they bloom. Sow chervil in pots again in early September to bring indoors when the first freeze threatens.

TIPS Buy new seeds every year, for old seeds are poor sprouters. Chervil can be used as a tasty green in salads, or as a garnish.

Chives
Allium schoenoprasum
Perennial

Mild onion-flavored chives should be in every container garden, for they are easy to grow, delicious, and produce pretty lavender flowers. Two 8-inch pots will furnish enough for the average family, including extra to freeze for use in the middle of winter. Place

plants in full sun in early spring (they can tolerate light frost). In hot climates, shift pots to a place where they will get afternoon shade in the summer. Keep soil moist, and fertilize every two weeks. Snip the narrow, tubular leaves when plants begin to grow actively. In the fall, pull the clumps apart into smaller bunches of two to five plants and repot these into new pots (about eight little clumps in an 8-inch pot). Bring a pot of chives indoors for winter harvest, for plants left outdoors will disappear until spring. Upright chives can be combined with other flowers and vegetables to make attractive container bouquets. Try them with yellow nasturtiums or annual verbena.

TIPS Cut back chives to 4 inches high two or three times during the summer to stimulate new growth. The pink flowers that form above the leaves in early summer are edible, too.

Cilantro/Coriander
Coriandrum sativum
Annual

The leaves are called cilantro, and the seeds (which are ground into a sweet, nutmeg-like spice) are referred to as coriander. This fast-growing dual-purpose herb grows best in spring and fall. Hot summer days make the plant go to seed quickly. Cilantro germinates fast and has a short lifespan, so sow a few seeds every three weeks for contin-

Cilantro.

Chives showing spring blooms.

Dill.

French Tarragon
Artemisia dracunculus
Perennial

French tarragon grows best in climates that are not too extreme in either summer or winter. Buy plants in spring, and set three of them in a 12-inch container. Give tarragon full sun, and keep the soil moist. Tarragon develops the best flavor in nutrient-lean soil, so fertilize lightly, if at all. This herb requires a period of winter dormancy, so it does not make a good winter houseplant. Instead, leave the plants outdoors through winter, preferably in a cold frame. In hot climates where French tarragon is difficult to grow, try Mexican marigold (see page 105), which has tarragon-like flavor but is much happier in warm weather.

TIPS Harvest tarragon in the morning when there are more essential oils present in leaves. Plants should be divided at least every two years, for they tend to weaken with time. Or root a few stem cuttings every summer and keep only the new plants.

uous leaf production. Start cilantro from seed sown directly into pots at least eight inches in diameter. Place in an area that receives early morning sun and afternoon shade. Keep soil moist and feed every two weeks. Remove flower buds to prolong leaf harvest, or allow plants to flower if you plan to harvest the seeds.

TIPS Choose cilantro varieties that seed catalogs list as "slow bolting" for the longest leaf production. Let the soil in containers dry out if you want plants to flower and produce seed.

Dill
Anethum graveolens
Annual

A dual-purpose herb, dill is grown for its flavorful leaves and its seeds. Both impart dill's distinctive flavor to foods. Sow directly into pots that are at least eight inches in diameter. Barely press seeds into the soil, for they need light to germinate. Place outdoors in a sunny spot after nightly temperatures are above 55°F. Keep soil moist and fertilize every two weeks. Dill flowers about 60 days after germination. For a continuous supply of flavorful leaves, plant more seeds every month. 'Bouquet' and 'Dukat' are fine varieties for containers.

TIPS Colorful caterpillars known as parsleyworms can strip all the leaves from a dill plant in hours. Either hand-pick the caterpillars and squash them (they don't bite), or move them to a roadside where they can eat wild Queen Anne's Lace until they are ready to pupate into black swallowtail butterflies.

French tarragon.

Garlic
Allium sativum
Perennial

Buy garlic bulbs from the grocery store or nurseries in fall or early spring, and divide them into individual, unpeeled cloves. Plant only the big outer cloves from garlic bulbs. Plant cloves pointed side up, 2 inches deep and 6 inches apart, in a container that is at least eight inches deep. Large boxes and tubs are ideal. Place in full sun, and keep soil moist until green shoots appear. Then water only when soil is dry one inch under the surface. Fertilize monthly. When the green tops droop and brown (about five months after planting), garlic is ready to harvest. Pull up and dry the bulbs in the sun.

TIPS In warm winter areas, plant garlic in late October and harvest in April. You can use tender young garlic leaves as a flavorful substitute for chives.

Garlic Chives
Allium tuberosum
Perennial

This easy-to-grow chive relative has flat leaves with a mild garlic-onion flavor. The beautiful white flowers that appear in late summer are edible, too, and have a light lilac fragrance. Garlic chives grow vigorously in hot or cold weather, and are always winter hardy. Set up to five purchased plants in a 10-inch container in spring, and place in full sun. Consistently moist soil and fertilizer twice a month are the only care needed. Divide clumps when containers become crowded, usually every two years.

TIPS Garlic chives have the best flavor when used raw or very slightly cooked.

Lavender
Lavandula angustifolia
Perennial

With gray leaves and fragrant purple flowers, lavender is a lovely addition to

Lemongrass.

any herb garden. Set out transplants in 10-inch pots filled with potting soil that has been amended with 3 or 4 tablespoons of lime. Place in full sun outdoors after the last spring frost, and allow plants to dry out between waterings. Fertilize monthly throughout the growing season. For fragrant sachets or potpourri, harvest flower spikes just as they begin to show color. Prune after flowering to keep the plants compact. In cold climates, take lavender indoors for winter, or bury the pots in mulch outdoors.

TIPS Scratch a tablespoon or two of lime in pots every spring to maintain the sweet soil lavender loves. A good container variety, 'Lavender Lady', blooms the first year from seed even in short season areas.

Lemongrass
Cymbopogon citratus
Tender Perennial

A tropical herb, lemongrass should not be set outdoors until nightly temperatures are in the low 60s. Choose a container at least 12 inches in diameter and depth, because the grass-like herb can grow to 4 feet and spread into a 6-inch clump at the base. Place in full sun. Let soil become dry between waterings, and fertilize lightly once a month. From Zone 7 northward, trim lemongrass back to 8 inches tall before frost comes, and store the pot in a basement or closet. In cool, low light conditions, the clump will turn brown and become dormant. Keep soil barely moist, and do not fertilize dormant plants. About a month before the last frost date in your area, put containers in a sunny window or under plant lights. When new growth appears, fertilize and water regularly.

TIPS Try growing lemongrass from a fresh stalk purchased at the grocery store. Stand the stalk in water until it sends out roots. Then pot it up and place it in a sunny spot.

Lemon Verbena
Aloysia triphylla
Tender Perennial

Tall and lanky in its natural state, lemon verbena needs at least a 12-inch container to support it. If harvested often, the fragrant lemon-scented herb will branch and become full and bushy. Place pots in full sun after the last spring frost. Some afternoon shade is appreciated in warm climates. Keep soil moist, and feed every two weeks. The short days of autumn will induce leaf loss, but this plant can survive outdoors to about 15°F if heavily mulched. In colder climates, bring indoors and place under plant lights for 14 hours daily. Or store containers in a cool, dry area until spring. While plants are semi-dormant, keep the soil barely moist.

TIPS Underplant lanky lemon verbena with short herbs and flowers to hide bare lower stems.

Mexican Marigold
Tagetes lucida
Tender Perennial

Also called Mexican tarragon, this member of the marigold family is a warm climate substitute for French tarragon. Set seedlings in 8-inch containers and place outdoors in full sun after the last spring frost. Keep soil moist, and fertilize every two weeks. Pinch new growth often to force branching. Mexican marigold is hardy

only to 28°F, so bring the plants indoors for winter.

TIPS The short days of autumn trigger the production of small yellow flowers.

Mint
Mentha species
Perennial

The herb comes in so many varieties that it's hard to choose just one. Peppermint (*Mentha piperita*) is the most common. There are scented ones such as apple, lemon and chocolate (which tastes like a chocolate-covered peppermint patty). Pineapple, another strongly scented variety, has cream and green variegated leaves. Bergamot tastes just like a cup of minty Earl Grey tea. Lavender has a perfume that mimics its name. There is even a blue-colored mint, 'Blue Balsam'. The smallest mint of all, Corsican, forms moss-like mats of minute, round leaves and is often used as a ground cover. All mints are invasive. They will quickly fill a container and then send out runners in every direction. Clip them off or pull up those that seem to miraculously appear in surrounding pots or soil.

Set transplants or rooted runners in eight-inch or larger pots in the spring after the danger of frost has passed. If possible, place the plants where they will get morning sun and afternoon shade. Too much shade will reduce the oil content of leaves. Keep pots constantly moist, and fertilize monthly. Bring indoors for winter north of Zone 7. If left outdoors in cold climates, store pots of mint in a cold frame or bury in mulch.

TIPS Mint flavors develop best if plants are fed with fertilizer high in nitrogen. Cut back plants in June and again in September to keep them tidy.

Oregano
Origanum vulgare
Perennial

Indispensable to Italian cuisine, oregano can be invasive since it sends out runners and reseeds itself. Its long stems can be fashioned into herb wreaths and then dried. Set up to three transplants in an 8- to 10-inch container, and place outdoors in full sun after the danger of frost has passed. Keep soil moist, and fertilize monthly. Trim runners often. Pots can be over-wintered in cold frames or buried in a foot of mulch. They can also be taken indoors and placed in sunny windows.

Marjoram (*Origanum majorana*) is a close relative of oregano and is grown in the same manner. However, it is less cold hardy and should be taken indoors for winter in climates where temperatures drop below 32°F. Marjoram leaves are finer in texture than those of oregano, and its flavor is different, too. All plants of this species tend to be slightly variable in flavor.

TIPS Both oregano and marjoram attract honeybees. Place their pots near container vegetables, such as squash, that require pollination. Marjoram is well suited for hanging baskets.

Oregano.

A Gallery of Container Herbs

Parsley
Petroselinum crispum
Biennial

There are two distinct forms of the parsley: Italian flat leaf, which has more flavor, and curled parsley, which is more decorative for garnishes. Both types of parsley produce loads of leaves their first summer, and flower the following spring. To assure a constant supply of leaves, start a few new seedlings every spring and fall.

An 8-inch pot will support two parsley plants. Set pots outdoors in a sunny spot around the time of your last spring freeze. Parsley easily survives light frosts. Keep soil moist and fertilize every two weeks. Growing parsley indoors during the winter usually requires supplemental light.

TIPS According to lore, parsley is an excellent companion for roses and tomatoes in containers, because it stimulates their growth. To speed germination of the seeds, soak them in water for 24 hours before planting.

Rosemary
Rosmarinus officinalis
Perennial

Most types of rosemary fall into two categories: upright and prostrate (or trailing). Choose a 12-inch or larger container that is at least a foot deep for upright types. Prostrate forms, which will eventually cascade over the sides of containers, can be planted in pots as small as 8 inches. Add 2 or 3 tablespoons of lime to the potting soil used to fill each

Rosemary with sage.

container. Place in full sun after the last spring frost. Let soil dry out between waterings, and fertilize only once every four to six weeks. In cold winter areas, bring plants indoors in winter.

TIPS Rosemary is an excellent insect repellent for moths. Scratch a tablespoon or two of lime into pots every spring to maintain the sweet soil rosemary loves.

Sage
Salvia officinalis
Perennial

The distinctive gray-green foliage of sage adds a soft color dimension to any collection of herbs. Sage grows tall and bushy and tends to sprawl, so choose containers at least 10 inches in diameter. Use a soil mix made from half peat moss and half commercial potting soil. Place outdoors in full sun and in an area where the air movement is good. Sage leaves don't like to be wet, and the drying effect of breezes will also deepen the plant's

Flat-leaf parsley.

Sage with bronze fennel.

giving it a silvery appearance. Creeping wooly thyme covers rocks and soil with fuzzy gray leaves. Citrus-scented thymes such as 'Lemon' are extremely fragrant. Some of the citrus varieties have variegated green and white foliage. There are herb-scented thymes, too, such as 'Caraway' and 'Oregano', which have the aroma and flavor of their namesake herbs.

Thyme has few requirements, but they must be met. Set three transplants in an 8-inch or larger container filled with a sandy potting soil. Place pots in full sun and keep soil moist. Fertilize every four to six weeks. Pots can be brought indoors, or you can bury the containers and mulch over them where winters are severe. Thyme will produce year-round in mild areas. Cut back growth by half in early spring. Replace plants every third year, or grow new ones from cuttings taken in early summer. After a couple of years, thyme plants tend to die out from the center.

TIPS To prevent mildew, top dress thyme pots with coarse sand. The oils that give thyme leaves their flavor are more concentrated if you pinch plants so often that they never have a chance to flower.

gray color. Let soil dry out between waterings, and fertilize every two weeks. Sage is cold-hardy and does not make a good house plant. Instead of bringing plants indoors, bury the pots in mulch where winter temperatures drop below 28°F or store them in a cold frame or cool garage or basement. Every spring, cut back the previous year's growth by half.

TIPS Dwarf sage (*Salvia officinalis nana*) has a low, neat growth habit that makes it the ideal sage for containers. Never add lime to pots of sage, for this herb prefers acidic soil conditions.

Thyme
Thymus species
Perennial

There are more than 100 species of thyme, and all of them are edible. Some form trailing, dense mats that are attractive when planted to spill over container edges or creep around woody stems in a container bouquet. Others grow 6 to 12 inches in height. English thyme (*Thymus vulgaris*) has the most robust flavor of all varieties. French thyme is more complex and aromatic. Silver thyme has gray foliage, but its leaves are edged with cream,

Thyme.

Chapter 9

VEGETABLES AND FRUITS

Bowls of freshly harvested salad greens, flavorful homegrown tomatoes and aromatic peaches dripping with juice—all container grown—are yours for the planting. Anyone can grow vegetables and fruits in containers as easily as gardeners with unlimited space. And, since container gardeners need not wait until soil is dry enough to cultivate in the spring, you can often stretch the growing season by getting an early start indoors.

One thing that all edible crops require is abundant sunshine. Most vegetables and all fruits require at least eight hours of direct sunlight daily to produce good tasting crops. Sunshine promotes high sugar content in fruits and some vegetables, and helps intensify more complex flavors, as well. The most shade-tolerant vegetables—lettuce and other leafy crops—can get by with four or five hours of sun.

The fine flavors found in a regular vegetable garden can be yours in containers. Here a salad garden shows that success is indeed beautiful.

CONTAINERS FOR VEGETABLES

All vegetables need containers big enough to support their root systems at maturity. Shallow-rooted vegetables such as lettuce, bush beans and peppers need a pot that is at least 8 inches deep, while the minimum depth for containers of tomato or eggplant is 12 inches. Larger containers hold more plants, and they are easier to care for than individual pots. See the *How Much Can You Grow?* box (at right) to get a good idea of how many vegetables you can grow in inexpensive plastic tubs with drainage holes punched in the bottom, or small and large window boxes. Old Styrofoam coolers, or wood crates lined with plastic, may also be used to grow vegetables.

Vining vegetables such as tomatoes, cucumbers and pole beans should be supported and trained to grow upward into the sun. You can let the stems trail over surrounding surfaces, but fruit quality is much better and disease is less of a problem when the plants grow up a trellis made of wire, string or nylon netting suspended between posts. Install the trellis when you plant or shortly afterward so it will be in place when it is needed.

UNDERSTANDING VEGETABLES

Most vegetables are annuals that race towards maturity, whether they are planted in the ground or in a pot. Some vegetables grow best in cool weather (spinach, lettuce, beets, broccoli) while others crave heat (tomatoes, peppers, cucumbers). In most climates, you can grow a few cool-weather crops in spring, then plant warm-weather veggies in early summer and finish the season with a second sowing of cool-natured plants for fall.

In all climates, get a jump on the spring growing season by seeding lettuce, carrots and other cool-season vegetables directly into containers a few weeks before your last frost. Place the planted pots outdoors on sunny days and bring them inside during freezing nights. When nights warm into the middle to high 50s, begin planting vegetables that need more heat. You will save your-

self weeks of growing time by starting with purchased bedding plants of tomatoes, peppers and even squash.

A constant supply of water, fertilizer and sunlight must be available to vegetables at all times. Whether you are an organic gardener or use chemical products, you can either use a slow-release fertilizer or mix fertilizer with the water you give to your plants. Detailed information on fertilizer choices can be found in Chapter 3.

Vegetables in containers produce more if their soil is kept evenly moist. Doing so may be difficult during the heat of summer, when a large tomato plant can consume 2 gallons of water daily. Drip emitter systems and soaker hoses on timers can be used to simplify watering tasks if you have a large collection of containers. Otherwise, be prepared to water every day in hot, dry weather. Also, the smaller the container, the faster it will dry out.

How Much Can You Grow?

SINCE VEGETABLES COME AND GO QUICKLY, it's easiest to grow carrots, cucumbers or whatever individually in one container rather than mixing things up too much. Here is an estimate of how many plants you can grow in various types of containers.

ONE LARGE TUB, 24 INCHES IN DIAMETER, WILL HOLD:
  50 carrots, radishes or onions or
  25 bush beans or beets or
  20 leaf lettuce or spinach plants or
  18 chard or celery plants or
  15 strawberry plants or
   5 cabbage, cauliflower or broccoli plants or
   3 okra, peppers, cucumber, melon or squash or
   2 eggplant or
   1 to 3 tomatoes, depending on your climate and the variety chosen

ONE SMALL TUB, 14 INCHES IN DIAMETER, WILL HOLD:
  25 radishes, onions or miniature carrots or
  12 bush beans or beets or
  10 leaf lettuce or spinach plants or
   9 chard or celery plants or
   7 strawberry plants or
   2 okra, peppers, cucumbers, cabbage, cauliflower or broccoli or
   1 squash, eggplant or tomato plant

ONE LARGE WINDOW BOX, 10 INCHES WIDE AND 3 FEET LONG, WILL HOLD:
  24 carrots, radishes or onions or
  16 bush beans or beets or
   9 leaf lettuce, pole beans or spinach or
   8 chard or celery plants or
   7 strawberry plants or
   2 cherry tomatoes, peppers, cucumber or squash plants

ONE SMALL WINDOW BOX, 6 INCHES WIDE AND 24 INCHES LONG, WILL HOLD:
  15 carrots, radishes or onions or
  10 bush beans or beets or
   6 spinach or leaf lettuce plants or
   5 chard or celery plants or
   4 strawberry plants

Gallery of Container Vegetables

Bean, Snap
Phaseolus vulgaris

Sow bush and pole bean seeds outdoors after the danger of frost has passed. Mass bush beans in tubs and pots at least 14 inches wide, and plant the seeds 1 inch deep and 2 inches apart in every direction. Bush beans do not mind these crowded quarters, but pole beans need more space. Seed them in a single row in a window box or other long, narrow container. At planting time, attach a 5- to 6-foot high trellis or frame to the container, or set the container next to a chain link fence. If you do not have a fence, run strings at 4-inch intervals from the top of the trellis (or the eaves of your house) to a heavy landscaping timber placed in front of the container. Push seeds 1 inch deep next to every string.

Keep soil evenly moist in containers, and fertilize once a month. Too much fertility limits pod production. Pick all beans while they are young and tender to promote more pod production. Bush beans will be ready to pick 50 to 60 days after planting and keep producing for a month or more. The first pole bean pods are ready about 80 days after sowing; healthy plants can produce until fall.

TIP For higher yields, inoculate bean seeds with nitrogen-fixing bacteria (sold in garden centers and catalogs as legume inoculant) before planting.

Beet
Beta vulgaris

Wooden barrel halves or large window-boxes will hold enough beets for the average family. Best grown from spring to early summer, beet seeds should be planted directly in containers a few weeks before your last spring frost. Plant seeds one-half inch deep and 2 inches apart and keep the container indoors for four days, covered with plastic or a piece of cardboard. As soon as the seeds begin to sprout, move the containers outdoors to a sunny place, but do cover with blankets if a late frost threatens. After two weeks, thin plants to 3 inches apart. Fertilize monthly and keep soil evenly moist. Roots are ready to eat 45 to 60 days after sowing.

TIP Keep containers very moist until beet seeds sprout, for drying out is the major cause of poor germination. Beet tops are both pretty and edible. Try them lightly stir-fried, like spinach.

Broccoli
Brassica oleracea Italica

Broccoli grows best in cool weather, so set out transplants in early spring and again in early fall in all regions except those with cool summers. Seeds can be started indoors about six weeks before the last spring frost or outside in August. Each broccoli plant will need the equivalent of 5 gallons of growing space, or a 14-inch pot. Fertilize every two weeks, and keep the soil moist. Broccoli is ready for harvest 50 to 80 days after transplanting, depending on variety. Harvest the central stalk before flower buds open (it will look like the broccoli you buy), taking only a 3-inch stalk with the head. Small side shoots form after the main head has been cut, and are ready to pick whenever you want them.

TIP Since broccoli roots release a toxin that inhibits the growth of other plants, do not combine them with other plants in large containers.

After the main head is harvested, broccoli produces a second crop of smaller florets.

Bok choy Chinese cabbage.

The best carrots for containers grow into plump balls or short cylinders.

Cabbage
Brassica oleracea Capitata

Cabbage is grown exactly like broccoli (see above), though it is hardier and can take temperatures well into the 20s without damage. Try growing miniature cabbages in containers. Two plants will fit into a 14-inch pot. Or you can grow non-heading cabbage by spacing plants only 3 inches apart. When you want them, simply pick and wash some tender young leaves, and use them like any other cabbage.

Chinese Cabbage (*Brassica rapa Pekinensis*) has similar needs, but it is usually damaged by temperatures below 28°F. Spring plantings are often not as productive as fall sowings made in August for harvest in October (or later in Zones 9 and 10).

TIPS To prevent insect damage, cover plants with spun polyester row covers. Light frost improves the flavor of cabbage.

Carrot
Daucus carota sativa

Any container that is at least 10 inches wide and deep will support a crop of carrots. Choose varieties that are short and stubby. Miniature carrot varieties can be grown in shallow pots only 6 inches deep. A light, sandy soil mixture is best. Sow carrots two weeks before the last spring frost, and again in late summer for a fall crop. When the

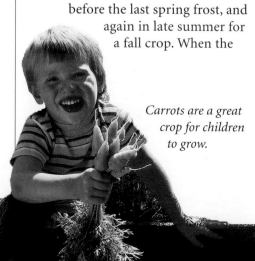

Carrots are a great crop for children to grow.

plants develop their first ferny leaves (a couple of weeks after germination), thin plants to 3 inches apart in every direction. Water daily if needed to keep soil moist, and fertilize weekly with a weak water-soluble fertilizer solution. The first carrots will be ready to eat 65 to 85 days after sowing.

GOOD CONTAINER VARIETIES Choose among short, stubby varieties including 'Short' n Sweet', 'Minicor', 'Amsdor' or 'Imperial Chantenay', and ball-shaped and mini-carrots such as 'Thumbelina', 'Little Finger', 'Partima' and 'Planet'.

TIPS Carrot seeds take up to two weeks to germinate, so be patient. To hasten seed germination, cover seeded soil with plastic or a piece of damp cardboard for four days after planting.

Cauliflower
Brassica oleracea Botrytis

Another member of the cabbage family, cauliflower likes cool weather. Set each transplant in a 5-gallon pot after the danger of frost has passed. Seeds can be started indoors six weeks before the last spring freeze is expected, or 10 weeks before the first fall freeze. Keep containers moist and fertilize every two weeks. Cauliflower is sensitive to boron deficiency. Heads are ready to harvest when the florets just begin to separate and get slightly ricey in appearance, about 50 to 65 days after transplanting.

GOOD CONTAINER VARIETIES 'White Corona Hybrid', 'Bambi', 'Violet Queen' (deep purple head).

TIPS For pure white cauliflower, pull leaves over developing heads and secure with string or rubber bands.

Celery
Apium graveolens

If you cannot find seedlings at local garden centers, start cool-natured celery seed indoors about six weeks before the last frost is expected. Set a single celery transplant into an 8-inch or larger pot, and place outdoors when nights remain above 45°F. If your summers are hot, plant celery in early fall and carry it over as a houseplant or outdoors in mild winter areas. Feed every week with water soluble fertilizer and keep pots very moist.

Plants are fully mature about 110 days after transplants are set out, but instead of waiting for a plant to reach full size, start pulling and using outer stalks when they are more than 6 inches long.

TIPS Blanch (whiten) celery stalks with a coffee can that has its bottom cut off. Place it around the plant after stalks are taller than the can.

Chard, Swiss
Beta vulgaris cicla

A close relative of beet, chard is grown for its large crinkly leaves with pretty white, red or yellow veins. Two to three weeks before the last spring frost is expected, sow seeds directly into containers that are at least 12 inches in diameter and depth. Sow seeds 1 inch deep and 4 inches apart. When seedlings are 6 inches tall, thin them to 8 inches apart. You can eat

Cucumbers.

the thinnings or carefully transplant them to mixed container bouquets. Keep the soil moist and fertilize every two weeks. Using a sharp knife, start cutting outer leaves about 60 days after sowing. If you harvest only two or three leaves at a time, you can pick from a single chard plant for up to three months.

GOOD CONTAINER VARIETIES 'Rhubarb' and several other varieties have showy wine red leaves that add color to container bouquets. 'Bright Lights' is a mixture that includes plants with pink, orange, yellow, red and green stalks.

TIPS Snap off flower stalks if they form to promote the production of more leaves.

Cucumber
Cucumis sativus

Bush-type cucumbers do best in pots that are at least 14 inches wide and 12 inches deep, or you can try

them in 14-inch hanging baskets. Vining types require a string trellis or a teepee-type trellis made of sticks. Sow seeds directly into containers after the last spring frost. Two weeks after the seeds sprout, thin plants to one or two plants per container. Keep soil moist and fertilize every two weeks. Cucumbers are ready to harvest about 60 days after seeding.

TIPS Harvest all fruits when they are young in order to help the plants produce for a long time.

Eggplant
Solanum melongena

Eggplant is one of those vegetables that does better in containers than in the ground, and the plants are pretty, too. Common eggplant diseases are not present in sterilized potting soil, so plants can flourish without disease problems. Container soil warms up much faster than the ground, and eggplant is a heat lover. Set out

Eggplant.

An assortment of lettuce.

purchased seedlings in late spring, when nights are nearing 60°F. Place a single transplant in a 12-inch wide or larger container. Fertilize every two weeks and keep soil moist. When hot weather arrives, it may be necessary to water pots twice a day to keep plants from wilting. Fruit is ready to harvest when it stops swelling and is still glossy, about 60 to 70 days after transplanting. Immature fruits are tastier than the fully mature ones.

TIPS To protect young plants from whitefly damage, drape them with polyester row cover or spray them with Neem or other insecticide.

Lettuce
Lactuca sativa

A cool-season crop, lettuce should be planted in early spring and again in early fall. Seeds will germinate in soil as cold as 40°F. To sow directly in large tubs or window boxes, sprinkle seeds over soil surface and press lightly. Some lettuce varieties need light to germinate. When plants are 2 inches tall, thin to at least 4 inches apart, and eat the thinnings or transplant them to

container bouquets. Pretty lettuce leaves mix beautifully with herbs and flowers. Grow lettuce in full sun, but provide afternoon shade when temperatures climb above 75°F. Heat turns leaves bitter. Fertilize every week, and keep soil moist.

GOOD CONTAINER VARIETIES 'Tom Thumb', 'Oak Leaf', 'Buttercrunch' and 'Little Gem' are but a few great varieties for containers.

TIPS When sowing seeds for your fall crop, allow the seeds to germinate indoors where it's cool.

Mesclun
Mixture of up to a dozen species of edible greens

The tender mix of baby lettuces, endives, mustards, cress, arugula, chervil and mache called mesclun

can be easily grown in 12-inch or larger pots and window boxes, indoors and out. Numerous mesclun seed blends are available at garden centers and from mail order catalogs. Some are mild while others have much sharper flavor. All should be harvested very young, about 35 days after sowing, so add fertilizer to the potting soil before you plant. Thoroughly mix one cup of high nitrogen fertilizer (9–3–7 pelleted fish meal or 10–10–10 fertilizer) into each 12-inch container. Water thoroughly, and then scatter seeds over soil and press in lightly. Following germination, containers can be placed outdoors two weeks before the last spring freeze is expected. Mesclun takes temperatures down to 26°F without damage, but cover pots with blankets if colder weather is likely. Keep soil constantly moist.

Start picking your mesclun when the leaves are 3 to 4 inches high. To harvest, cut outer leaves with scissors, taking care not to damage plant crowns. Plants should produce four more cuttings, taken at ten day intervals. Sow new pots of mesclun every two weeks for a continuous supply of salad greens.

TIPS Harvest early in the morning and cut only enough for one meal; flavor is best when mesclun is consumed within 12 hours of cutting. Never let plant leaves get taller than 6 inches, because they will stop producing new leaves.

Okra
Abelmoschus esculentus

Also called the gumbo plant, new varieties of okra allow northern and southern gardeners to enjoy this edible hibiscus relative in containers. Add one to a container floral bouquet and take advantage of the lovely yellow flowers with burgundy centers. Red stemmed cultivars such as 'Burgundy' bear brilliant red pods for more color.

Start seeds indoors about a month before night temperatures are expected to stay above 50°F. When nights are that warm, carefully transplant okra into container bouquets or large individual pots, disturbing the roots as little as possible. Position containers against a fence or wall that can block winds that might topple the tall plants, or plant short varieties such as 'Lee'. Fertilize every two weeks, and keep soil slightly moist. Pods begin to develop about 60 days after seeds are sown. In warm weather, they will reach picking size (3 to 4 inches long) in only a few days. Cut pods from plants with a sharp knife or pruning shears.

TIPS All okra plants have spines that cause itching, so wear a long-sleeve shirt and gloves when picking.

Onion
Allium cepa

Onions to use as scallions are a cinch to grow in containers. Simply plant purchased seedlings or dormant sets (tiny dried onions) 1 inch apart in any potting soil or container, and within a month they will be ready to pull. If you want big bulb onions, space the plants at least 4 inches apart in containers at least 8 inches deep. Fertilize once a month, and keep containers lightly moist. When leaves begin to yellow (about a hundred days after transplanting), pull away soil from bulbs, exposing the top half. Lift them when leaves turn completely brown. Cure them in the sun for a couple days after pulling, and store them in a cool, dry area.

Bunching Onions (*Allium fistulosum*), also called multiplying onions, form mild-flavored thick stems instead of bulbs. They are perennials and will produce bumper crops of scallions in spring and fall. Bunching onions divide themselves to form clusters, and some strains develop bulblets atop tall stalks following

Bunching onions, or scallions.

flowering. To keep a strain going indefinitely, divide clumps in both spring and fall.

TIPS Purchased onion seedlings that are larger than a pencil often do not bulb well, but make great scallions. Bulb formation is dependent on day length, so pick short-day onion varieties in the south and long-day ones for the north.

Pea
Pisum sativum

Peas grown for peas (called shell peas), those grown for pods (called snow peas) and tender peas that produce both sugary peas and plump pods (called snap peas) all are grown the same way. Because they love cool weather, they are among the first vegetables planted in spring. All peas form vines that need support. Window boxes and other long narrow containers are ideal, because either a trellis (for tall climbers) or a series of twigs (for short-vined ones) can be positioned next to plants. You can also place your pea container against a wire fence. Young peas have no problem with frost, so sow seeds outdoors two weeks before the last spring freeze. Fertilize once a month and keep soil moist. Harvest when pods are plump and still tender, about 60 to 75 days after sowing. You should be able to feel small peas inside the pods. Keep picking to promote more production.

TIPS To boost yield before planting seeds, inoculate with nitrogen fixing bacteria (legume inoculate available in small packets at garden centers).

Pepper
Capsicum annuum

From the hottest habañeros to the sweetest chocolate bells, peppers were made for container growing. Start seeds indoors about six weeks before

Caribbean pepper.

the last spring frost is expected, or purchase transplants. Amend potting soil with a tablespoon of Epsom salts per container. Stick a couple of unburned wooden kitchen matches in each pot, too. Peppers require lots of magnesium, and the sulfur in the matches helps to neutralize salt buildup. Set transplants in 2-gallon or larger containers, at least 12 inches wide and 8 inches deep.

Place peppers outdoors in full sun after night temperatures are above 45°F. Sweet peppers dislike temperatures above 85°F and should be shaded in the afternoon during the summer. Hot peppers, on the other hand, love sun and heat and produce more fruit during hot weather. Keep all plants constantly moist to avoid heat stress, and fertilize weekly with half-strength water-soluble fertilizer. When blossoms form, give plants an extra magnesium boost to promote large peppers by spraying leaves with a weak solution of one teaspoon Epsom salts dissolved in one quart of warm water. Repeat every two weeks as long as there are flowers on plants. Peppers are

ready to harvest 55 to 85 days after transplants are set out. Containers can be brought indoors when autumn freezes threaten.

TIPS Hot peppers will be hotter if you let the soil in their pots dry out occasionally, but watch for leaf drop as an indication that soil is too dry.

Radish
Raphanus sativus

Fast-maturing radishes are best grown in the cool seasons—spring and fall. Sow seeds in an 8-inch or larger container and thin plants to at least 1 inch apart a week after the seeds sprout. Keep soil evenly moist and feed weekly with a water soluble fertilizer. Only three to four weeks after sowing seeds, your first radish should be ready to pick. In cool climates, plant radishes once a month for continuous production.

TIPS Pick radishes as soon as they plump up for the mildest flavor and best quality. They keep in the refrigerator up to one month.

Spinach
Spinacia oleracea

Spinach is easy to grow in containers provided it gets plenty of nitrogen and the soil is slightly alkaline. Before planting, mix 2 tablespoons of lime and a quarter cup of blood meal or other high nitrogen fertilizer into each 8-inch pot. Plant spinach in early spring and again in late summer, when days are cool and short in length. Start seeds directly in containers indoors a month before the last spring frost and set them outside as soon as they sprout (they actually like light frosts). Space plants 3 to 4 inches apart in window boxes or large tubs. Keep soil moist and feed with a water-soluble fertilizer or fish meal emulsion every two weeks. Start harvesting outer leaves from plants about 40 days after sowing.

TIPS If plant centers turn yellow, spinach needs more nitrogen. Fall-sown spinach will continue to grow after the weather turns cold.

Squash
Cucurbita pepo, Cucurbita maxima, Cucurbita moschata

The squash family is large and varied, and includes tender crooknecks, hard-shelled butternuts and even pumpkins. All are grown in the same manner, and all except huge Hubbards and giant pumpkins do well in containers. Small pie and miniature pumpkins are excellent container choices. Vining squash types require wooden barrel halves or other large tubs and trellising. Six-foot high lengths of wire mesh can be formed into cylinders and placed in the middle of containers to hold the vines. Peg the wire to the soil with stakes for added stability. Or place tubs against a trellis or fence to which you can tie the vines. Bush types need 12-inch or larger pots for each plant. A wooden barrel half can hold three plants spaced equal distance apart.

Sow seeds directly into containers, and thin to the strongest seedlings after they have two sets of leaves. Keep soil constantly moist, and fertilize every two weeks. Summer squash is ready to pick 50 to 60 days after sowing. Winter squash and pumpkins can take up to 120 days to mature. After rinds are very hard, cut them from the vine, leaving a 2- to 3-inch

Zucchini squash in a hanging basket.

stem, and cure in a warm, dry place a week or two before storing.

TIPS Squash flowers need up to four visits from insects for pollination, or you can hand pollinate flowers with a paintbrush (see page 119). Tie up the vines of large winter squash and pumpkins with old pantyhose or strips of soft cloth.

Tomato
Lycopersicon esculentum

If you plant only one container vegetable, make it a tomato. There are three types of tomato plants: determinates, which grow to about 3 feet and stop; semi-determinates, which can reach 5 feet before they stop growing, and indeterminates, which are really vines that grow until disease or frost kills them. All fruit from determinate and semi-determinate plants is harvested within a 30 day period. The harvest goes on all season with indeterminates. Plant the type that suits your needs.

Any tomato will flourish in a container. The ideal size pot is a 14-inch diameter tub that holds ten gallons of soil, but vining varieties bearing small cherry tomatoes can be

Stakes and wire cages support a heavy crop of tomatoes.

grown in 10-inch wide hanging baskets. Add a half cup of time-release fertilizer to the soil in each container. Push support stakes or tomato cages into tubs before planting. Indeterminate tomatoes may outgrow cages in warm climates, so position their containers next to a trellis or fence for later support.

Start tomato seeds indoors about six weeks before the last spring frost, or purchase transplants from garden centers. Strip off all leaves on transplants except the top four leaves, and plant them deep in containers so that only the remaining leaves are above the soil line. Roots will form along buried stems. Place containers outdoors in full sun after the last frost. Tomatoes cannot tolerate cold or frost, for they are tropical plants. Keep soil constantly moist, but avoid wetting the leaves. Dry foliage deters fungal diseases. Fertilize every two weeks. After the first fruits form, scratch 2 or 3 tablespoons of blood meal or 2 teaspoons of ammonium sulfate into soil. The nitrogen boost makes for bigger fruit.

GOOD CONTAINER VARIETIES Cherry tomatoes such as 'Sun Gold', 'Sweet Chelsea', 'Gardener's Delight' and 'Yellow Pear' are container mainstays.

Also try compact varieties such as 'Better Bush' and 'Husky Gold', as well as full-sized 'Celebrity', 'Better Boy', or 'Big Beef'.

TIPS Wrap tomato cages with spun polyester row cover or clear plastic to protect tender transplants from wind and cold; leave covers on until plants are 2 or 3 feet tall. Hang red Christmas tree balls on tomato plants just before they begin to ripen their fruit to fool birds. They will peck at the hard balls, go away and leave the later-ripening tomatoes alone.

Vine-ripe tomatoes.

'Tiny Tim' tomatoes.

GROWING FRUITS IN CONTAINERS

Small fruits such as melons and strawberries are naturals for containers. Their needs are easily met, and disease problems are minimal. Citrus and bananas, which grow outdoors only in tropical climates, can be grown in any regions if kept indoors through winter.

Because of their eventual size and weight, fruit trees and fruiting shrubs need large sturdy containers such as wooden barrel halves or large plastic pots or tubs. Clay pots in sizes that will support trees are costly, heavy and subject to cracking in cold weather.

Whatever type of container you choose, the size should be just 2 or 3 inches wider than the roots of the plant. If you start with a bareroot tree, the first pot should be about the size of a 5-gallon nursery pot. Move trees up from that size to containers that are the size of a bushel basket over a two- to three-year period. Citrus should be started in a container not much bigger than its rootball and moved up to slightly larger pots yearly. Fruiting trees and shrubs are best purchased in late winter or early spring, when they are emerging from winter dormancy and ready to make rapid growth of new leaves, stems and roots.

When selecting apple and stone fruit (cherries, peaches and plums) trees for containers, shop for dwarf varieties. Dwarf trees generally will grow to a maximum of 10 feet or less, versus 18 to 35 feet for semi-dwarf or standard trees of the same variety. Dwarf trees begin producing fruit sooner than standards, too. Genetic dwarf varieties are preferable to those that are dwarfed by being grafted onto special rootstocks, for genetic dwarfs usually need less pruning and are more disease-resistant. However, either grafted or genetically dwarf trees will do well in the controlled environment of a container.

Apple and stone fruit trees require precise pruning at planting and every winter thereafter. When buying tree cultivars developed especially for container culture from mail order nurseries, pruning instructions are usually provided with the plants. Otherwise, ask your county extension agent for free printed material on how to prune and train various fruits, or find a book in the library.

REPOTTING FRUIT TREES

After two or three years in one container, citrus, fig, apple and stone fruit trees should be repotted. In late winter, while the plants are still dormant, examine the container's drainage holes. If roots are growing out of the holes, it's time to repot and prune. Citrus should be repotted and pruned after fruit is harvested.

Turn containers on their side and gently pull the rootball out. It may be necessary to tap pots and loosen soil at the edges with a long knife. Using a sharp, serrated knife, remove about 25 percent of the roots by slicing off thin strips from all around the root mass. Then pry the lowest few inches of remaining roots apart from the bottom so that they butterfly outward very slightly. Prune branches, too, removing about 25 percent of the growth.

Clean containers before repotting trees. A stiff brush and a weak bleach solution (a tablespoon household bleach to a quart of warm water) will sanitize and remove salt residues on pots and tubs. Add fresh potting soil and set the tree back in its container. If moving trees up to bigger pots, select one that is only slightly larger than the previous one. Newly cut roots tend to rot in containers that are very large because there is so much moisture present. Citrus roots are particularly vulnerable to this problem.

WINTER CARE

Tropical fruits such as bananas and citrus must be wintered indoors, except in the mildest climates. From Zone 7 northward, figs need to be wrapped up in blankets or kept in a cool garage through winter to keep the bearing buds from being damaged by cold weather.

Fruit trees that lose their leaves in winter and become dormant in winter (called deciduous trees) can remain outdoors in regions where temperatures remain above −10°F. From Zone 6 northward, place your dormant fruit trees in a sheltered area against a building. In very cold climates, protect tubs by wrapping them with several layers of burlap and newspaper, or two layers of plastic bubble wrap.

Early spring is a perilous time for any fruit tree, particularly those in containers. Flowering begins earlier with trees in tubs, because the soil warms faster. A freezing night can easily kill all potential fruit. Be prepared to move containerized trees in bud or bloom to sheltered areas or indoors when frost threatens.

Chilling Choices

*D*IFFERENT VARIETIES OF TREE FRUITS have different chill hour requirements, and those requirements must be met before the trees will flower and set fruit successfully.

Chill hours are defined as the number of hours that temperatures are below 45°F in the course of an average winter. Warm areas in the South and along the Pacific Coast receive as few as 200 chill hours, while northern climates receive thousands of chill hours. Tags on trees sold at garden centers will list chill hour requirements. They are also listed in fruit tree descriptions in mail order catalogs. Before buying fruit trees, consult your county extension agent or garden center to find how many chill hours your area receives.

Gallery of Container Fruits

Apple
Malus pumila

Apples should be planted in pairs, because two cultivars are usually needed for cross pollination (fertilization that creates fruit). Ask your county extension agent or consult catalogs to find out which dwarf apples that grow in your area will pollinate each other. Or plant dwarf trees that have two or more varieties grafted to one tree. Consider columnar, spur-type apple trees that are 2 feet wide and grow to only 8 feet. They are especially adapted to containers and require little or no pruning.

Fertilize apples monthly from the time their first flowers appear until late summer. Scratch in one to two tablespoons of 10–10–10 fertilizer or one pound of composted manure. Water thoroughly after feeding. Keep soil moist at all times.

TIPS Dwarf apple trees will bear fruit in their second or third year. So will columnar types. To grow the biggest, juiciest apples possible, thin small green fruits to 6 inches apart on branches, or one to each short stubby spur on columnar trees.

Banana
Musa acuminata

With wide tropical leaves and rampant growth, bananas are gorgeous additions to any container garden even without their fruit. When they do fruit, homegrown bananas are extremely sweet and flavorful. Dwarf varieties like 'Rajuapuri' will bear their fruit in about seven months; 'Dwarf Cavendish' takes about a year. Most dwarfs grow no more than 6 feet in height before their flower stalk appears and fruit develops. Use a tub at least 14 inches in diameter for bananas.

Bananas will survive to 28°F if protected, but they're sluggish in growth below 50°F. Plants thrive indoors under fluorescent grow lights and can be moved outdoors just as soon as nights are in the 50s. They love hot, south-facing windows, too, where they can receive sun all day.

A banana tree's life is over after it has fruited, but suckers or pups will appear at its base. Cut down the old plant and select the strongest pups for next year's crop. Set pups or small plants firmly into soil and water. Let the containers become somewhat dry and begin watering regularly after you see new growth. Feed plants every three months with a half cup of time-release fertilizer formulated for tropical plants.

TIPS Let fruit ripen on the plant for the best flavor. When bananas turn bright yellow, they are ready to pick. Banana flowers attract bees and hummingbirds, so group plants with others that need pollination.

Blueberry
Vaccinium corymbosum, Vaccinium ashei

Blueberries need acidic soil, plenty of moisture and good drainage—all things that are available in a container. Select highbush types in the north and rabbiteye blueberries for southern areas. Plant two cultivars for pollination. A knowledgeable nursery-worker or your county extension agent can tell you the names of the best varieties for your area.

Use a large tub or 16-inch pot for each plant. Fill containers with a mix of half potting soil, half dampened peat moss and a half cup of fertilizer formulated for acid-loving plants. To help keep the soil moist, mulch around the plants with a 2-inch blanket of rotted leaves, pine needles or old sawdust. Blueberries need little fertilizer, for their roots are fine and shallow and easily damaged by strong fertilizers. If the leaves become pale, make a light application of a slow-release fertilizer for acid loving plants.

Pick off blossoms the first year and allow only a small crop to mature during the second season. Crops will be larger and of better quality thereafter. After the third season, lightly prune plants in late winter by removing thin, weak growth and old wood. The largest berries are borne on fresh new canes.

TIPS For the sweetest fruit allow berries to remain on bushes for a day or two after they turn blue. Use netting to defend your crop against birds; cover plants as soon as the berries begin to turn pink.

Preventing Pollination Problems

EXCEPT FOR LEAFY GREENS AND ROOT CROPS, most vegetables and fruits develop from fertilized flowers. In a large garden, insects and wind spread pollen where it needs to go, but in small container plantings, you may need to assist in the pollination process.

With tomatoes and peppers (which are normally pollinated with help from wind), gently tap open flowers twice a day to move pollen to flower anthers. Cucumbers, squash and small melons develop male and female flowers, and only the female flowers (which appear a little later than the males) are capable of setting fruit. You can identify female flowers by looking for a tiny green fruit located behind the base of the flower. To lend a helping hand to pollination, use a small paintbrush or cotton swab to collect pollen grains from the male flowers. Immediately rub the pollen into the centers of the female flowers. They are the ones with tiny fruit at their base. To be certain that your mission is accomplished, transfer pollen from at least four male flowers to each female flower.

Cherry
Prunus avium, Prunus cerasus

In addition to their succulent fruit, cherry trees put on a floral show every spring that will light up any garden. Many cherry cultivars need pollinators, but there are several dwarf varieties that are self-fruitful and well suited to containers. These include 'Garden Bing', 'Compact Stella' and 'Lapins' sweet cherry, and 'Dwarf North Star' sour cherry. Fertilize cherries monthly from the time the first blossoms appear until late summer by scratching in one quarter cup of 10–10–10 fertilizer or 2 pounds of composted manure. Water thoroughly after feeding. Keep soil moist at all times.

TIPS Sour cherries are sweet enough to eat fresh if allowed to ripen fully on trees. For best storage, pick cherries with their stems attached.

Citrus
Citrus species, Fortunella species

Small citrus varieties such as calamondins and kumquats make wonderful houseplants. Bigger citrus such as oranges and lemons do, too. Their fragrant waxy white blossoms perfume any house in winter. Citrus was the first container-planted edible

Lemon tree.

in history. The Romans grew them in clay pots, and 17th century European rulers constructed vast glass buildings called orangeries to house their citrus treasures.

Plant new citrus shrubs and trees in late winter or early spring, using a container slightly larger than the tree's rootball. Fill the container with potting soil and add two tablespoons to a half cup (depending on tree size) of citrus fertilizer that contains chelated iron and micronutrients. Place the tree's graft union (the knobby area near its base) 2 inches above the soil line.

Fertilize trees every two weeks with a water soluble fertilizer during the growing season. If leaves turn pale green or yellow, scratch in a tablespoon of ammonium sulfate or a quarter cup of blood meal. When growth stops, stop fertilizing. The following spring, scratch in a cup of citrus fertilizer and water thoroughly. Let the soil surface in containers dry out between waterings, but don't let the trees become stressed for water. If they do, they will drop their leaves and take moisture out of developing fruit. If seriously stressed, they will even drop their fruit.

Kumquats.

Lemons.

Orange tree.

Citrus trees surround an entryway.

Orange: Robertson Navel, Diller, Bouquet
Orangequat: Nippon.

Fig
Ficus carica

Citrus should be root-pruned and repotted every two or three years. No other pruning is needed, except for the removal of suckers—new shoots that grow from base of trees where they have been grafted. Overwinter trees indoors in areas where winter temperatures dip below 28°F, being careful to keep the plants away from heat and air conditioning vents which dry out leaves. Hold back on fertilizer until new growth appears. If citrus trees blossom while indoors, take a cotton swab and transfer pollen from one flower to another to make sure fruit sets.

TIPS Trees grow fast in hot, humid climates, and may need root pruning and repotting annually. Most citrus varieties will hold mature fruit on the tree for up to a month, so you can pick it as you need it.

GOOD CONTAINER VARIETIES
Kumquat: Meiwa, Nagami
Lemon: Eureka, Improved Meyer, Ponderosa
Lime: Bearss
Limequat: Tavares
Mandarin Orange: Calamondin, Kimbrough, Dancy, Owari

'Washington Navel' oranges.

Fresh figs are a taste delight no one should miss. Most gardeners think of figs as semi-tropical plants, but these tough little trees (or multi-stemmed shrubs) can take freezes and even survive in dark, cold basements during frigid northern winters. Start with a container-adapted variety such as 'Celeste', 'Brown Turkey' or 'Italian Honey', all available from mail-order catalogs and garden centers. Set it in a light-colored pot that holds at least 10 gallons of soil. Fig roots are sensitive to heat, so also plant trailing flowers or herbs at the base of the tree so that they will cover the container sides by midsummer.

Figs appreciate time-release fertilizers, mixed into the soil at planting, that give them small continual doses of nutrients. In summer, fertilize once a month with half strength water-soluble fertilizer. Figs sometimes fruit in their first year. Two crops a year are the norm—a light one in late spring and heavier second

Fig.

crop in fall. Figs are ready to pick when they are slightly soft and start to bend at the neck.

TIPS Figs must ripen fully on trees and can be stored in the refrigerator for only four or five days. If some limbs appear dead in early summer, prune them off.

Melon
Cucumis melo, Citrullus lanatus

Cantaloupes, honeydews and small watermelons all can be raised in large wooden barrel halves or 24-inch wide tubs that have 6-foot wire mesh cylinders or trellising attached or anchored within the container. The trick is to train vines upward and secure developing fruit with cloth slings to support them. Old nylon pantyhose are great for slings, because they expand with the developing melons.

Fill containers with potting soil that has been enriched with five pounds of composted manure. Start seeds indoors in cool spring areas or seed directly into containers after nights are in the 50s. Three plants should be spaced equally around the container. Fertilize every two weeks with a water-soluble food and scratch in one cup of 10–10–10 fertilizer after vines begin to run. Keep soil constantly moist.

Melons are ready to harvest 70 to 120 days after sowing. Cantaloupe are ready when a gentle tug will separate them from the vine. Honeydew and French charentais are ripe when their skins turn yellow. It's more difficult to pick a ripe watermelon. The most fool-proof method is to observe the nearest tendril (the curlicue) to the melon stem. When it turns completely brown, the melon is probably ripe.

TIPS For the sweetest melons, fertilize plants with a boron solution (one tablespoon household borax dissolved in a quart of warm water) when the vines start to climb. Because melons require heat to grow and to make sweet fruit, position containers against a south-facing wall in cool climates.

Peach
Prunus persica

The most popular of homegrown fruits, peaches can be had two years after planting a dwarf tree in a tub. Most are self-pollinating, so you have to plant only one. Pick a variety that needs the number of chill hours your

Peach.

area receives. Nectarines and plums are similar and are grown in the same manner.

Set bareroot trees or potted plants in wooden barrel halves or 24-inch wide tubs in early spring, after the last frost. Mix a half cup of 10–10–10 fertilizer into the soil at planting and water thoroughly. Feed every two weeks with a water-soluble fertilizer while there is active growth. Keep soil evenly moist.

TIPS Thin fruit on branches to stand 6 inches apart when peaches are the size of a quarter. Shop mail-order catalogs for genetic dwarf peaches suited to the available chill hours in your climate.

Pomegranate

See Pomegranate (on page 133), in Chapter 10.

Pomegranate with thyme.

Strawberry
Fragaria species

Growing strawberries in containers is a breeze. A 6-inch clay pot will easily support one strawberry plant, because roots are shallow and don't mind being cramped. However, it makes more

A well-filled strawberry jar.

sense to mass a number of plants together for ease of care and bigger harvests. Large tubs, window boxes and clay strawberry jars are ideal.

Everbearing strawberries produce fruits all summer, while spring-bearing varieties produce all at once in late spring or early summer. Try different varieties until you find the right one for your climate and exposure. If you start with a certain variety and find it is not what you want, simply start over with new plants of another variety the following spring.

Set out plants, spacing them 6 inches apart, in late winter about three weeks before the last frost is expected. From Zone 7 southward, you can also set strawberries in containers in the fall. As soon as new growth appears, begin feeding plants every two weeks with a balanced water-soluble fertilizer. Keep soil moist at all times. Mulch plants with an inch of shredded bark or straw to conserve moisture and keep berries clean.

TIPS Protect ripening berries from birds and squirrels with netting or spun polyester row cover.

Chapter 10

❦

ROSES, SHRUBS AND TREES

Long-lived shrubs and trees bring structure and continuity to the container garden season after season. Their size and height make them perfect as living backdrops for groupings of smaller plants. A special tree or shrub may be just what your container collection needs to make the scene look more like a garden and less like a jumble of pots. If you want to evoke the feel of a lush woodland in your container garden, or grow evergreens so you will have living, green plants to enjoy through the winter, you will need some shrubs or trees.

You may also find that certain shrubs and trees, including roses, grow better in containers than they do in the ground. Plants that benefit from perfect drainage, and others that withstand winter better when protected from frigid wind and icy soil are especially good candidates for containers.

A section of clay pipe makes a fine permanent home for a yellow shrub rose.

With proper care, you can grow almost any type of shrub or small tree in a container. However, just as with perennial flowers, restricting the root run of large plants tends to limit their size. For this reason, a Japanese maple tree that grows to 14 feet in the ground may only grow to half that size in a container. Container culture has a similar dwarfing effect on many shrubs.

CHOOSING CONTAINERS

Since shrubs and trees are quite massive when they are in full leaf, it is usually best to avoid tall containers that are easily toppled. Instead, looks for sturdy pots with broad bottoms, or planting boxes that can be moved about on rollers. Weight is always a consideration unless you plan to leave your container-grown shrub or tree in the same place indefinitely. Concrete or stone containers planted with boxwoods or junipers, for example, are too heavy to move—and may be too heavy for a terrace or balcony. Growing the same plants in lightweight plastic pots can cut their weight in half.

With some shrubs and trees, container depth is as important as width. Roses grow best in containers at least 16 inches deep, and most trees need planters closer to 18 inches deep or deeper. However, dogwoods, azaleas and other woody plants with shallow roots can be grown successfully in containers that are low and wide. In general, you will find that shrubs or trees with a strongly upright growth habit, such as bamboo, pillar type junipers and floribunda roses tend to need deep pots, while plants that show strong sideways growth or an umbrella-shaped limb pattern are more at home in broad, comparatively shallow containers.

ROMANCING THE ROSE

Gardeners adore roses, which are quite willing to grow in well-drained containers. Since roses need constant moisture in summer and the pots must be moved to a cold yet sheltered place in winter, most gardeners grow them in lightweight plastic pots at least 16 inches deep. Roses also seem to like the fact that plastic pots do not become hot and dry like clay pots do. A good quality potting soil or soilless mix is fine for roses, or you can make up your own planting soil by mixing together equal parts of good garden loam, peat moss, sand and thoroughly rotted manure. All roses prefer a near neutral pH of 6.5, so you may need to add lime to soil mixtures that include acidic ingredients like peat moss or leaf mold. To many gardeners, part of the fun of growing roses is tinkering with the soil to find the elusive perfect mixture.

Roses need thoughtful pruning if they are to grow and flower well. Exact pruning procedures vary with climate and the type of rose being grown. It is always a good idea to prune away the small limbs that have produced faded flowers, for the next flowers will emerge from new growth. Pruning off the old tips helps to force out this new growth. Most roses are pruned rather severely in either fall or spring, depending again on cultivar and climate. In very cold areas you can go ahead and prune back container-grown roses by at least half in fall. Where winters pose less of a threat to the plants, delay your heaviest pruning until late winter.

Roses become dormant in winter, and they benefit from being left in a cold place until spring. From Zone 6 northward, you can help your container-grown roses survive winter by placing the pruned plants against a wall and then loosely binding up the mass of plants with several layers of burlap or plastic bubble wrap. In Zones 7 and 8, practices for winter protection are seldom more elaborate than mounding up pine straw or sawdust over the pots, or simply moving the plants to a cold, unheated outbuilding during unusually frigid spells of weather.

CHOOSING ROSES

There are more than a dozen major types of roses, and all of them with the exception of huge climbing and rambling roses can be grown in containers. At the same time, some species and cultivars have a proven track record of great performance when grown in pots. A short list of these roses follows, sorted according to type, along with general guidelines for growing them. Since fragrance is a big plus to container gardeners, all of the roses named here are known for their delightful scents.

Hybrid Tea Roses

These are the classic long-stemmed roses with large, vase-shaped buds and big blossoms. They are prickly, angular plants. For containers, look for cultivars known for their cold hardiness and disease resistance, such as 'Miss All-American Beauty' (pink), 'Double Delight' (pink blend), 'Olympiad' (red) and 'Tropicana' (coral).

Hybrid tea roses are sold when they are dormant. At retail stores, the selection is usually best in late winter. Buy the best quality roses you can find, and shop early so you can get the plants settled

Rosy Recommendations

THE AMERICAN ROSE SOCIETY RATES the performance of roses around the country and gives cultivars a numerical rating based on their composite scores. A list of varieties with the highest scores (the break point for very superior cultivars is 8.5) is published annually. To see the most up-to-date list, go to the Society's web page at www.ars.com and review it. This list also appears in the Society's booklet titled Handbook for Selecting Roses. The cost is $4. You can order this booklet directly from The American Rose Society, P.O. Box 30,000, Shreveport, LA 71130; phone (318)938-5402.

into pots before the little buds along the stem produce their first leaves. Hybrid tea roses are usually sold with bare roots packed in damp peat moss and then wrapped tightly in burlap or plastic. When you plant them, make sure any bulging graft union sits well above the soil line. Keep the soil constantly moist but not wet. When the plants start developing green stems and leaves, begin fertilizing at least every third time you water with a water soluble fertilizer. Some rose devotees prefer to add a small amount of fertilizer to the water every time they water from spring until late summer.

Floribunda Roses

Tough and adaptable, floribunda roses produce clusters of small but well-formed blossoms, and they often rebloom several times during the summer. Floribundas are generally hardier and more disease resistant than hybrid tea roses. Excellent floribundas for containers include 'Iceberg' (white), 'Europeana' (red) and 'Sexy Rexy' (pink).

Plant and grow floribunda roses exactly like hybrid teas, but be prepared for a pleasant surprise. Hybrid teas may produce larger flowers, but floribundas are usually prettier plants. Although they do repeat bloom, floribundas usually bloom very heavily in late spring, and lightly thereafter. When in full bloom, one healthy floribunda rose will captivate the container garden.

Miniature Roses

Miniature roses grow to only about 15 inches tall, and are usually not grafted. Healthy plants on the brink of bloom are widely available at garden centers in spring, and a few, such as 'Red Cascade', have an almost vining habit perfect for hanging baskets. The flowers of all miniature roses resemble very small hybrid teas. 'Giggles' (pink), 'Rise 'n' Shine' (yellow) and 'Pacesetter' (white) are highly regarded for their vigor and fragrance.

Miniature roses are the simplest type of rose to grow in containers, and can be

Miniature rose.

purchased as bedding plants in little four-inch pots. To transplant them to nine-inch pots, baskets or other containers, push them out of their nursery pots from the bottom and dunk the roots in room temperature water to loosen them a bit. Settle each plant in its new pot at the same depth that it grew in its nursery pot. Fertilize at least every third time you water.

Tree Roses

Tree roses are grafted plants in which a cluster of stems taken from showy hybrid tea roses or heavy-flowering floribundas are grafted onto the tops of tall, hardy rootstocks. Most of the classic hybrid teas and vigorous floribundas are available as tree roses. Tree roses are among the most treasured types of roses to grow in 14-inch containers, since they provide the means to grow tempera-

mental hybrid teas in a small space, and of course they have a breathtakingly formal form.

Since the top of a tree rose is little more than a cluster of grafts, tree roses require careful winter protection. In cold-winter areas, they are best moved in late fall to a cold garage or other sheltered place where temperatures will not drop below 20°F. Before forgetting about them, wrap each plant lightly in an old blanket. As far south as Zone 8, tree roses may need to be brought into a garage or barn when temperatures drop below 25°F. Most tree roses are hardier than this, but the plants are much too costly for unnecessary risks. Needless to say, keeping tree roses through winter is much easier when you are working with containers than when you are growing them in the ground.

Species Roses

Some old non-hybrid roses are too huge for containers, but two deserve special consideration. The so-called butterfly rose, *Rosa chinensis* 'Mutabilis', produces single flowers all summer in changing shades of yellow, orange, pink and red. Another species rose, *Rosa moyesii* 'Geranium', is covered with bright red flowers in spring, followed by a heavy crop of bright red berries, or hips, which persist until frost.

Species roses are interesting shrubs, and no two of them are exactly alike. Unless you have been advised otherwise by a knowledgeable gardener, grow species roses just as you would hybrid teas or floribundas, but prune them lightly until you learn more about each plant's natural habit of growth. Also, do not be too quick to judge a species rose in its first year at your home. Although highly bred roses often put on their best show the first year after planting, a well adapted species rose is more likely to be a strong long-term performer.

Other Choices

Local rose societies flourish in many towns and cities, and the knowledge and experience shared by rose growers who live close to you is always the best way to discover rare jewels in the huge world of rose cultivars. Antique roses will grow in pots, as will the latest English roses and romantic old damasks. Ask around to find local gardeners who are also interested in unique and historical roses and will share their knowledge with you.

Tree rose.

SHRUBS AND TREES

Bushy shrubs and upright trees are usually chosen to serve very specific purposes in the container garden. While many shrubs do produce beautiful flowers, they are best thought of as texture plants that bring structure and contrast to container gardens. We take trees for granted when they grow in the ground, but put them in a container garden and they become an instant focal point. You can also move potted trees around to use as backdrops to help spotlight smaller plants that are nearing perfection. Since the sheer size of these biggies can easily overwhelm the small scale of a con-

tainer garden, you will probably need but a few well chosen shrubs or trees.

Hundreds of different types of shrubs and trees can be grown in containers, including both evergreen and deciduous types of plants. Deciduous plants shed their leaves in fall and become dormant until spring. Hardy evergreens stand firm through ice and snow and help bring cheer to the coldest winter days.

When shopping for either type of plant, the safest bets are those already growing in containers. However, evergreens are often sold with their roots wrapped in a ball of burlap and soil. Simply remove the burlap before setting the plant in its pot, but retain the soil packed around the plant's roots. If the plant has a knot in its main stem just above the soil line, it has probably been grafted. When placing a grafted plant in a pot, be sure that the graft union is at least an inch above the top of the soil.

All shrubs and trees make most of their new growth in spring and early summer, and few need repotting more often than every two to three years. However, refreshing the top inch or two of soil in the containers is highly recommended. With most shrubs and trees, you can use a large spoon to gently scoop off the top inch of soil, and quickly replace it with fresh material. If the roots of the plant are very near the surface, as is usually the case with azaleas and boxwood, simply place a layer of fresh soil atop the roots without disturbing them.

A Gallery of Shrubs and Trees for Containers

The following 17 shrubs and trees are among the most useful ones in container gardens. All will thrive in containers that are at least 14 inches deep and equally wide. Special soil or pruning requirements are given in the plant profiles.

Aucuba
Aucuba japonica 'Variegata'
Zones 6 to 8

Also known as gold dust plant, variegated aucuba produces large, glossy green leaves with golden yellow specks. This shrub grows best in shade and flourishes even in very dark shadows cast by buildings and privacy fences. Fill containers with a peaty soil-less mix or another potting medium that holds moisture well. In large containers, try underplanting aucuba with ferns. Prune aucuba only to control its size. North of Zone 7, trim aucuba lightly in fall, clean the plant well, and keep it indoors in a cool room as a winter houseplant.

Azalea
Rhododendron hybrids
Zones 4 to 10

The princess of spring-flowering shrubs, azaleas can be grown in containers in areas where they run into trouble in the ground. Available in a huge range of colors, azaleas are top choices for partial shade. Give any azalea a wide container that drains well, and set the plant high, so the roots are barely covered, using a peaty potting medium. Fertilize lightly once a month, using a half dose of an acidic fertilizer. Positively soak containers when watering them to help leach out accumulated salts. If the plant's leaves begin to turn yellow, they may need iron. The quickest fix is to spray the plants with an iron solution (available at garden centers). Prune azaleas only to trim off awkward stems. Since azaleas vary widely in their winter hardiness, it is best to shop for plants

Azalea, trained as a standard.

locally. North of Zone 6, many hardy azaleas will drop their leaves in winter, and produce new foliage the following spring.

Bamboo
Arundinaria and *Bambusa* species
Zones 6 to 10

Bamboos are actually gigantic grasses. There are dozens of species of bamboo and all except the giant types may be grown in large containers. The strongly upright plants are valuable for screening or framing views while bringing a tropical touch to the container garden. Cultivars that form dense clumps, such as *Bambusa multiplex* 'Golden Goddess', are usually the best choices for containers. This species is hardy only to about 20°F, so you may need to bring it indoors for short periods during the winter. However, all bamboos resent sudden changes in temperature, and are best left outdoors as much as possible. They will grow in any well-drained soil, and require dividing at least every three years.

Dwarf bamboo.

Boxwood
Buxus species
Zones 4 to 9

The same boxwoods used as foundation plants in home landscapes can be used as anchor evergreens in the container garden. Begin with plants of any size and move them to slightly larger containers yearly until

Boxwood with English ivy.

they reach the size you want. Thereafter, prune at least twice a summer to shape the plants. From Zone 7 northward, stop pruning in late summer, for new growth is easily damaged by winter weather. Shop for plants locally to find the best adapted cultivars for your area. Boxwoods like a moist potting soil and at least a half day of strong sun. They resent having their roots disturbed, and are best grown by themselves in their own containers.

Dogwood
Cornus florida
Zones 5 to 9

America's favorite flowering tree is easily grown in large, broad containers that are seldom moved. A slow-growing hardwood tree by nature, dogwoods need several years to reach full size, which seldom exceeds 12 feet or so when they are grown in pots. Provide a soil-based mixture that includes plenty of peat moss or leaf mold, for dogwoods must be kept lightly moist at all times. Prune only to remove damaged limbs. Carefully selected nursery-grown trees usually flower earlier and more heavily than wild ones. Red-flowered cultivars also are a little slow, and may not start blooming until they have been settled in for two or three years. Repot dogwoods only when they need it, about every three years. Once trees reach mature size, their roots are best left undisturbed.

Dwarf Alberta Spruce
Picea glauca 'Conica'
Zones 2 to 8

If you want a hardy Christmas tree to grow in a pot on your patio, look no further than the dwarf Alberta spruce. This hardy evergreen grows so slowly that it may take a full decade to mature to seven feet. Meanwhile, you may never need to go near it with pruning shears, fertilize it only occasionally and

Dwarf Alberta spruce.

water it when it gets dry. Purchase plants in spring or fall, and set in pots only a few inches wider than the rootball, using any potting soil that drains well. Repot every two or three years. As the tree grows, you may want to add heavy rocks to the bottom of the pot or planter to give it extra weight.

Flowering Maple
Abutilon hybridum
Zone 8

This plant is not a maple at all, but a flowering shrub from South America. Yellow flowers appear from early summer onward on thin branches. Abutilon thrives in full sun in cool climates, but partial shade is best where summers are hot. Any good quality potting soil that holds moisture well is fine. In summer, pinch off the tips of long branches to encourage bushy growth and the development of new flower buds, and fertilize every two weeks. North of Zone 8, prune plants back by half, clean them thoroughly and keep them as indoor houseplants through the winter. Repot

each spring, adding small annual companion plants such as impatiens to the container composition.

Heather
Calluna vulgaris
Zones 5 to 7

Scotch heather, also known as ling, is a small evergreen shrub with stiff, scaly foliage. The flowers that appear in late summer or fall on the mound-shaped plants may be white, yellow or pink, depending on cultivar. Foliage color also varies between green, gold and chartreuse. Many container gardeners collect several varieties, grow each of them in an individual pot, and display them together. Heather likes a very lean, acidic potting soil such as a mixture of equal parts peat moss, sand and soil. Fast drainage is crucial. Prune plants back by about one-third in winter, after the flowers fade. Fertilize lightly in spring and midsummer with an acidic fertilizer such as those labeled for use on azaleas.

Heath
Erica carnea
Zones 5 to 9

Winter heaths are especially valuable in the container garden because they bloom from midwinter until spring, when few other plants show any color. There are many other kinds of heaths, including tender ones that are used as ground covers in very mild winter areas. However, container gardeners usually stick with hardy evergreen winter bloomers, including 'Springwood White' (white), 'King George' (red) and 'Alan Coates' (pink), all of which grow only 6 inches high and up to 18 inches across. Cultivars that bloom pink or red usually have tinted leaves. Grow heaths just like heathers, but trim them back after the flowers fade in spring. Although they grow best in acidic soil, heaths tend to be a little more tolerant of alkaline conditions compared to heathers.

A Gallery of Shrubs and Trees for Containers

Hibiscus
Hibiscus rosa-sinensis
Zones 9 to 11

A tropical evergreen shrub, hibiscus is best grown as a winter houseplant and then moved outdoors to a sunny spot after the last spring frost is but a memory. Dozens of varieties are available in a huge range of bright colors. All are easy to grow in 14-inch pots filled with any good potting soil. Water regularly, whenever the soil appears dry, and fertilize monthly during the summer. Prune lightly to shape plants any time. In spring, just before you move your plants outdoors, cut them back by about one-third to force out new flowering branches. Repot every other spring. In years when the plants are not repotted, gently replace the top inch of soil in the container with a fresh supply.

Holly
Ilex species
Zones 3 to 9

The same tough nature that makes hollies popular as foundation shrubs may win them a place in your container garden. For year-round enjoyment, choose a hardy evergreen type that is adapted in your climate. To grow hollies that produce berries in cold climates, you will need both male and female plants of a hardy deciduous type such as the native *Ilex verticillata* species. Evergreen Japanese holly does not have traditional holly leaves or berries, but is hardy to Zone 5. Numerous cultivars are evergreen in Zones 6 to 8. All hollies grow best in roomy pots filled with a soil mixture that retains moisture well. Mulching over the tops of the pots helps keep the shallow roots from drying out.

Hydrangea
Hydrangea species
Zones 6 to 9

Hydrangeas are popular shrubs for container gardens, valued for their

Pink hydrangea.

French hydrangea.

lush green or variegated foliage and large, showy blossoms. Big-leaf hydrangea, *H. macrophylla*, blooms pink in alkaline soil and blue in acidic soil. In addition to this species, there are many others worthy of inclusion in a container collection. All hydrangeas grow best in containers placed in partial sun and kept constantly moist. In early summer, six-inch long stem cuttings may be rooted in a sandy medium to form new plants. In cold-winter areas, prune back plants by half their size in late fall after the leaves have been shed, and keep them in a cool protected place through the winter. In Zones 6 and 7, wrap plants with burlap before hard freezes commence. Hydrangeas bloom best on the previous year's growth, which is easily damaged by temperatures below 20°F.

Japanese maple
Acer palmatum
Zones 4 to 9

This is the top tree for container culture, for no other tree can equal its grace and beauty in a container-sized package. There are numerous named grafted cultivars, which vary in size between three and 15 feet and may have red or green leaves. You can also grow seedling trees in pots, which tend to stay less than 10 feet tall when their root run is restricted. All Japanese maples show brilliant fall color and grow in sun or partial shade in a wide range of climates. Set trees in a heavy planter at least 16 inches deep in early spring, and mix a handful of slow-release fertilizer into the potting mixture. Allow the plant to grow freely for a year, pruning only to shape the canopy. Japanese maples usually need repotting only every three years.

Juniper
Juniperus species
Zones 3 to 9

The feathery evergreen foliage of juniper makes them a top choice for containers. The most useful ones are upright, pillar-type cultivars that bring dramatic vertical accents to the container garden. They are especially useful near entryways or in the corners of sunny patio or terrace gardens. Tremendously winter hardy and easy to grow, junipers also come in forms that grow into low, dense bushes, or twisting, almost contorted silhouettes. Depending on the cultivar, foliage may be green, gray or creamy yellow. Most large garden centers sell locally adapted varieties in spring. Grow junipers in a rather heavy, soil-based potting mixture, and keep them in full

Dwarf Japanese maple.

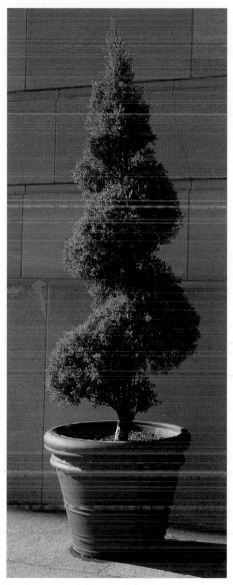

Juniper, pruned to a triple twist.

sun. Repot every year or so, disturbing the roots as little as possible.

Mugo Pine
Pinus mugo var. *mugo*
Zones 2 to 8

This unusual pine looks like a cross between a shrub and a tree. It grows to less than five feet tall, and usually produces numerous low branches that create the shape of an irregular spiking mound. Plant mugo pine in spring or fall in a broad container at least 16 inches deep. A rich but sandy potting soil is best. Water regularly for the first year, and thereafter only when the container becomes very dry. With copious sunshine, a mugo pine will quickly grow into a living evergreen sculpture.

'Pomegranate
Punica granatum
Zones 9 to 10

Pomegranate cultivars suitable for containers do not set fruit, but they do produce a long succession of beautiful orange, peach or yellow flowers. They demand strong sun and alkaline soil that dries quickly following heavy rains. Depending on cultivar and pot size, plants may grow to between two and six feet tall. Trim lightly to shape plants, and protect them from hard freezes by moving them to a cool, protected place in early winter. When wintered in a cool garage, plants can be grown where winters are much too cold to keep them outdoors. Flowering pomegranates exhibit bright yellow fall color just before the leaves fall. A few selections are evergreen in very mild winter climates.

Wisteria
Wisteria species
Zones 6 to 9

Wisterias are really vigorous vines, but in containers they are best trained into standards—umbrella-shaped shrubs atop a stout, woody trunk. If you enjoy pinching and pruning, you will love this plant. Set purchased plants in containers at least 16 inches deep filled with any good potting soil, and stake the main stem to hold it steady. When it grows to the height you want (usually about three feet), pinch off the top and any stems that have formed near the bottom of the trunk. Continuous pinching and pruning of the plant's canopy will result in a well-formed umbrella shape that blooms heavily in spring. Young plants may be fertilized monthly to support fast growth, but stop fertilizing after the plants are two years old.

Wisteria.

Chapter 11

❉

THEME CONTAINER GARDENS

Like any other kind of garden, a container garden can be created to accent special features and themes that give it a strong sense of a specific style. In this chapter, we will look at a few of the most popular types of theme gardens, which are basically container gardens in which a special vision is carried out through the selection and placement of plants. Theme gardens are fun to create and require no more work than any other type of container garden. However, they do limit your choice of plants, and at the same time set an appealing stage for distinctive features that you may find especially enjoyable, such as bonsai trees or shrubs in an Asian style garden, or a tub garden complete with goldfish and aquatic plants.

To introduce you to these special theme gardens, we will look at the parts of each and how they fit together into a whole. You can also get great ideas for

A beautiful bonsai collection shares a deck with peppers and tomatoes.

Asian Simplicity

developing your own theme gardens by visiting other gardens and nurseries in your area.

ASIAN SIMPLICITY

Whether they grow in containers or fill a large park, Asian gardens use a few carefully chosen plants, placed to create a simple meditative scene. There are many ways to design an Asian style container garden, and entire books are devoted to this art. Symbolism and suggestion often play major roles in Asian garden design, which means that an Asian style container garden is much more complex than it appears.

The **site** for an Asian garden needs to be sunny for most of the day, and large enough to accommodate both plants, passageways and a place for thoughtful relaxation.

Containers for Asian gardens are typically low and broad, so that they are hardly noticed after they are filled with plants, stones or water. Colors are dull

earth tones in shades of green, gray or brown.

Tough little **trees**, trained and pruned using bonsai techniques, look like miniature versions of very old trees—and they may be decades old, in fact. They are often trained to grow asymmetrically, so that it appears that a persistent wind has caused them to grow a certain way. A single bonsai tree brings motion to a container garden. At the same time, it works as a meditative focal point that symbolizes the spiritual presence of the forest.

Flowering shrubs such as azalea or pomegranate may be grown as bonsai, or simply kept neatly trimmed and celebrated for their natural forms and their blossoms. They are grown in broad, low containers, and the top of the soil, which shows beneath the shrub, is an important part of the composition. It may be mulched over with moss, or perhaps paved with carefully selected pebbles.

Flowering plants are chosen to celebrate various seasons, such as iris in spring, roses in summer and chrysanthemums in fall. In an Asian garden, foliage color and form is as important as the colors that come from flowers.

Ferns and mosses that dramatize the earth underfoot may be prominently represented, usually in their own simple containers strategically embellished with selected stones.

Rocks or stones are as visible as plants in many Asian gardens. In a small container garden, a single heavy stone may be placed so that it feels like a craggy mountain. Smaller stones or gravel, arranged around the base of the large stone, may be used to complete the picture.

Water is often an intregral part of an Asian garden. In a container garden, this may be a small water garden or simply a shallow trough that is filled with water to create a reflective surface. Or a small pump may be used to gently trickle water over a stone, recapture it in a

placid reservoir, and then recirculate it again and again.

The sky is part of the container composition. Seating should be arranged so that the garden can be viewed with the sky as part of the picture.

WINDOWSCAPES

Windowboxes are all about color. European in origin and mood, windowscapes can be used to bring grace and beauty to stark buildings, can accentuate the colors used in other parts of the yard or can be put to work growing fragrant herbs in close association with cascading flowers. From inside the home, windowboxes are an easy way to view flowers up close, along with the bees and butterflies who visit them on warm days. Seen from the street, windowboxes can be formal and refined or cheerful and whimsical.

Since windowboxes must fit onto window frames or ledges, they are almost always rectangular in shape. Most

container gardeners use boxes which in turn hold plastic liners. The actual planting and growing is done in the liners, which are slipped into the boxes in spring and removed in fall, before they can become heavy with ice. As explained in Chapters 2 and 3, the main requirements for windowboxes are that they be firmly attached and permit excess water to drain away. If they are attached to high windows, you also must be able to water them from inside your house via an open window.

Transforming a windowbox into a windowscape is easily done using plants that vary in size and texture, as outlined below. When filling windowboxes that are attached to the front of your house, it is usually best to use the same planting scheme in all of the boxes. However, if you have two stories of windows to adorn, there is no law against using a slightly different planting design for the boxes on the first and second floors provided the colors coordinate.

Here are some of the most popular ways to turn windowboxes into container gardens. Whenever you create a windowscape, bear in mind that you will be crowding plants together so that they grow almost on top of each other. When the plants completely fill the box with roots, you will need to provide water and fertilizer more often than you would if they were growing in roomier quarters.

Tall upright flowers give structure to the composition, and provide one of the focal colors. Light colors often show up best. Plant at least three flowers that will grow to be twice as tall as the depth of the box, but leave a little space on either end for small companion plants. In full sun, excellent tall bloomers include geraniums, miniature roses or snapdragons. If the box will get more than a half day of shade, salvia, coleus or caladium are better choices. Basil and rosemary are also fine upright plants for edible windowbox compositions.

Windowscapes

Soft mounding plants provide texture and color to fill the front and center of the box. Many flowers can do this job, but some of the best are petunia, verbena and dwarf marigold. In shady locations, impatiens is unsurpassed for filling boxes with lush foliage and colorful flowers. Also consider gray-foliage plants such as dusty miller or lamb's-ear, as well as frilly varieties of leaf lettuce.

Cascading plants soften the edges of the windowscape and visually accentuate the pull of gravity. They are the magic touch that makes a windowbox look like a hanging garden. Variegated vinca vine or long pieces of ivy are perfect for this job, or you can let blooming plants such as lobelia or sweet alyssum spill over the sides of the container. Thyme is the herb of choice for dressing the edges of boxes planted with herbs or vegetables.

CONTAINER WATER GARDENS

Small water gardens that sit atop the ground, often called tub gardens, are an irresistible focal point in a container garden. In a small yard or courtyard, you also have the option of setting your water garden down in the ground, but above-ground tubs are equally attractive and functional. In all situations, water gardens impart a cool mood along with a strong dash of the tropics. Best of all, container water gardens are great fun to create and quickly become a source of daily fascination.

The **site** for an aquatic garden must be absolutely level, and should receive sun for at least half of the day. In very warm summer climates it is possible to keep a water garden that is shaded most of the day, but most aquatic plants grow best in full to partial sun.

Containers can be large clay pots with their drainage holes sealed with a silicon plug, iron kettles with flat bottoms, half barrels or boxes built of wood in which a flexible plastic liner is fitted that holds the water. If you intend to keep fish in your tub garden, it is best to line these types of containers with two layers of heavy grade black plastic or special liners made for barrels. Fish-safe barrel liners designed to last 20 years cost less than $25. Pond supply stores also sell decorative plastic containers for water gardens, which at first glance may look like large clay bowls or half barrels. These plastic containers are inexpensive, lightweight and do not require any type of liner. They are also easy to clean for winter storage.

The container depth can be as shallow as 7 inches if your plan calls for growing only plants. The inclusion of fish, however, requires a depth of at least 18 inches, for fish need a cool place to hide on hot days.

Fish are both functional and decorative in a tub garden, for they control mosquitoes while putting on a never-ending show. The easiest fish to keep are small comets, a plain but very adaptable type of goldfish. Larger, showier fish such as koi need more room than is available in small tub gardens. A half whiskey barrel that holds 80 gallons of water will support three or four small goldfish along with three or four types of aquatic plants.

A **pump** for filtration or pushing water through a small fountain is an option, but not a necessity in a small tub garden. A lot of water movement can interfere with the growth of some types of aquatic plants, so limit fountains to small spouts or trickles rather than big sprays. Filtration is seldom needed in tub gardens where healthy plants are present, for the plants handle much of the work of keeping water clear and in proper chemical balance.

Plants for water gardens usually are planted in pots which sit below the water's surface. They vary in their preferred depth, and you may need to set some of the pots on bricks or another type of support to keep them at the proper depth. A half-barrel tub garden provides enough room for one small water lily and two or three other types of plants. In addition to potted water plants, you can include floating plants in your water garden. Consult water garden catalogs and visit water garden stores in your area to get the best recommendations for plants.

Chapter 12

PESTS AND DISEASES IN CONTAINER GARDENS

Plants grown in containers are bothered by the same pests and diseases as other plants. However, these problems are more easily controlled in small container plantings, for there are usually a limited number of host plants. All insects and diseases require the presence of an appropriate host, and they are usually able to infect a very narrow range of plants. For example, pea aphids are not uncommon on sweet peas, but this is a highly specialized type of aphid that cannot digest the juices of any plant except peas. Diseases have the same narrow range of acceptable host plants. Powdery mildew on zinnia, for example, cannot spread to non-related plants, because a highly specialized strain of the fungus causes powdery mildew on zinnias.

Use the chart that follows to help identify specific problems that may

Keeping container plants healthy is the most important way to prevent problems with pests and diseases.

develop with your plants. Some of the symptoms listed here are not insects or diseases at all, but rather physiological problems that may be due to improper watering or fertilization. All are easiest to correct when the problem is spotted early and steps are taken to remedy the problem right away. With insects, this might mean simply pinching off affected plant parts or giving the plants a good cleaning. Safe and effective controls are described for each malady.

INSECT PROBLEMS

Aphids

SYMPTOMS AND CAUSE Tiny insects are clustered on plant stems, mostly on tender young growth. They may be green, black or gold, depending on species. When you try to touch them, they barely move. A few of the largest ones may have tiny wings. These are *aphids*, which feed by sucking plant juices. There are different species of aphids for different plants. Aphids weaken plants but seldom kill them.

PLANTS AFFECTED Of plants commonly grown in containers, sweet peas, chrysanthemums, lettuce, broccoli, fruit trees and iris are most likely to to host aphids.

WHAT TO DO If plants have only a single cluster of aphids, simply pinch off that plant part and dispose of it. If the insects are scattered over plants, as is sometimes the case with leafy greens, spray the plants thoroughly with plain water or insecticidal soap. Do not apply insecticidal soap until evening during hot, sunny weather or the plants' leaves may be injured.

Slugs or Snails

SYMPTOMS AND CAUSE Small holes with smooth edges appear in plant leaves overnight. Upon close inspection, you may find faint shimmery trails left behind by either *slugs* or *snails*. These creatures are not insects, but are among the most common pests seen in container gardens. They hide beneath pots

Slugs and snails.

during the day, and move upward to feed on plants during the night.

Plants affected

Slugs and snails feed on a wide variety of plants, including hostas, snap beans, lettuce and just about any type of small seedling or young plant.

What to do

The most direct solution is to remove the slugs or snails by hand. Wear a thin glove (such as a latex medical exam glove), and go out at night and pick them off. Drop them in a cup containing saltwater to kill them. Early in the morning, gather slugs found hiding in the dark beneath containers.

Whiteflies

SYMPTOMS AND CAUSE Plant leaves show very tiny white specks, which are so numerous that the leaves appear to be a lighter color than normal. If you gently swish the leaves, very tiny white moth-like creatures called whiteflies take to the air. A few moments later, they settle back upon the plants, and feed by sucking juices from tender stems and leaf undersides.

PLANTS AFFECTED Azalea, impatiens, begonia and many types of vegetable seedlings and shrubs may be bothered by whiteflies. In most areas whiteflies are most common from midsummer to fall, but on the West Coast they can be a problem all summer long.

WHAT TO DO As soon as whiteflies are identified, spray plants thoroughly with insecticidal soap. Apply in the evening or

during cloudy weather, or leaves may be slightly damaged. Early intervention is important to keep the populations from growing, but in some areas whiteflies may be so well established that weekly treatments with insecticidal soap are needed.

Caterpillars

SYMPTOMS AND CAUSE Plant leaves may show holes, or the leaves may be damaged along their edges. At the same time, there may be small pebbly bits of dark green or black "frass" beneath the plants. This is the waste of *caterpillars*, which eat plant leaves. Caterpillars are the larvae of moths and butterflies, and vary in color and size, depending on species.

PLANTS AFFECTED Trees, shrubs, tomatoes and many other plants may serve as hosts for specific species of moth larvae.

WHAT TO DO On small individual plants, the easiest cure for caterpillars is to simply pick them off. When a number of caterpillars are feeding on a tree or shrub, you can control them by spraying the plants thoroughly with an insecticide that contains *Bacillus thuringiensis*, abbreviated Bt, which is a naturally-occurring bacteria that makes caterpillars sick but is harmless to humans. Thuricide and other liquid Bt formulations do not leave visible residue on plant leaves. Don't harm caterpillars if you have a butterfly garden.

Tent caterpillars.

Japanese beetles

SYMPTOMS AND CAUSE When rosebuds form, they become the scene of a feeding orgy by half-inch long beetles with metallic copper bodies marked with green and showing small white dots on their sides. These are *Japanese beetles*, a serious pest of rose and many other plants grown in the East and Upper South. The range of this pest is gradually moving westward.

PLANTS AFFECTED Rose is the great favorite of Japanese beetles, but they can also cause serious damage to hibiscus and many other plants.

WHAT TO DO The least toxic pesticides for Japanese beetle control are made from neem, derived from the bark of the neem tree. If you are growing roses where this pest is common, apply a neem-based insecticide to your plants weekly as soon as the beetles appear. They normally emerge in early summer and disappear six to eight weeks later.

Scale

SYMPTOMS AND CAUSE Stems, twigs and sometimes leaves show small discs, usually about one-eighth inch wide, which are firmly attached to the wood. You can scrape them off with your fingernail, but they do not attempt to move. These creatures are called *scale*. They feed by sucking plant juices, and give off a sticky substance the often turns into deposits of black mold.

PLANTS AFFECTED Ferns, holly and many trees and shrubs, including fruit trees and roses, can become infested with scale. There are different species of scale that feed upon different plants.

WHAT TO DO For very small problems, simply coat the scale colonies with vegetable oil using a cotton swab, being careful not to get the oil on plant leaves. For larger problems, look at garden centers for products described as light hor-

ticultural oils. These oils are safe to apply to plants listed on the product label. They kill scale (as well as aphids, whiteflies and other small sucking insects) by suffocating them. You will need a small pressure sprayer to apply light horticultural oil

DISEASE PROBLEMS

Rose black spot

SYMPTOMS AND CAUSE When rose leaves show small, roughly circular black dots on them, they have become infected with a fungus called *rose black spot*. If you are unsure, use a magnifying glass to examine a few spots. Each spot will have a softly fringed edge.

PLANTS AFFECTED Rose is the only plant seriously affected, and susceptibility varies with cultivar. In general, hybrid

Rose black spot.

tea roses are the most susceptible, and shrub roses are more resistant. However, any rose can develop problems with this disease. Resistant roses may be slightly weakened by black spot. Very susceptible roses may lose so many leaves that they are nearly killed.

WHAT TO DO First, do what you can to prevent the problem. Clean up and dispose of all rose leaves at the end of the season. When a small outbreak develops, promptly clip off the leaves and spray plants with a mixture made from 1 teaspoon baking soda, 1 quart water, and a few drops of dishwashing detergent. If the problem becomes epidemic, turn to an approved fungicide and follow label directions exactly.

Botrytis

SYMPTOMS AND CAUSE Following a spell of wet weather, petunia blossoms may show tan spots where drops of water remained for several hours. These spots are caused by a fungus called *botrytis*. Another form of the fungus causes strawberries to rot as soon as they ripen. Affected strawberries show a fuzzy mold on the fruits.

PLANTS AFFECTED Petunia blossoms, strawberry fruits and a few other plants are susceptible to various forms of this fungus.

WHAT TO DO Since botrytis needs wet conditions to flourish, the first step is to move the plants to a place where they can stay dry for a few days. Chemicals are available to control botrytis, but they are seldom, if ever needed in container gardens.

Powdery mildew

SYMPTOMS AND CAUSE White powdery patches on plant leaves are the definitive sign of *powdery mildew*. This fungus weakens plants slowly by destroying leaves, but it seldom kills them. However, leaves with powdery mildew are not attractive.

PLANTS AFFECTED Rose, phlox, zinnia, cucumber and pea are sometimes affected by powdery mildew. Many cultivars are resistant. The words "mildew resistant" on plant tags or in catalogs usually refer to powdery mildew resistance.

WHAT TO DO Plant resistant cultivars when you can. Also pinch off leaves that

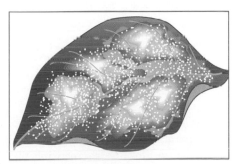

Powdery mildew.

show this disease and dispose of them. If a certain cultivar always shows symptoms of mildew, get rid of it and switch to a new one that does a better job of resisting this disease.

Early blight

SYMPTOMS AND CAUSE Tomato leaves show numerous brown spots on the leaves closest to the ground. If you look at the spots closely, you will see that they are somewhat angular in shape, and have faint concentric rings within each spot. These spots are caused by a fungus, and are commonly called *early blight*. Badly affected leaves gradually shrivel to brown, yet remain attached to plant stems.

PLANTS AFFECTED Tomatoes and potatoes are susceptible to this disease. On tomatoes, the spots seldom appear near the tops of the plants, and may be limited to the lowest limbs. Affected plants continue to grow and produce good quality fruits.

WHAT TO DO This fungus must have damp leaves or the spores cannot germinate. Avoid wetting leaves when watering late in the day or during the evening. Sometimes it also helps to clip off the lowest leaves at the first sign of spotting. No tomatoes are truly resistant to early blight, but varieties with flat rather than curled leaves tend to tolerate the disease best.

OTHER PROBLEMS

Root rot

SYMPTOMS AND CAUSE Plants shrivel and die. Frequently this process goes slowly, with leaves curling along their edges at first. However, very young plants affected with *root rot* may collapse and die overnight. Root rot can be caused by a large number of different fungi that live in the soil.

PLANTS AFFECTED Numerous plants can develop root rot, and very young ones are the most likely to be damaged. You can also accidentally invite problems by

setting plants in unclean containers, or by using old soil that has been colonized by invisible fungi.

WHAT TO DO Use a sterile soilless mix when starting seeds, along with very clean containers. If a single plant in a container bouquet shows signs of root rot, remove it along with the soil right around its roots, and fill the spot with a new plant of a different species.

Nitrogen deficiency

SYMPTOMS AND CAUSE Plants grow slowly and the leaves are light green or yellowish. Since plants require nitrogen to grow lush green leaves, these symptoms are the classic sign of *nitrogen deficiency*.

PLANTS AFFECTED Any plant can develop this problem. It is very common with plants grown in containers, for every time you water, you wash out nutrients in the soil. Also, most soilless mixtures contain very few plant nutrients, and the plants quickly deplete any nitrogen that is present.

WHAT TO DO To turn plants around in a hurry, douse them with a weak mixture of fish emulsion fertilizer. Seriously deficient plants will take up nitrogen through their leaves and through their roots. Begin feeding plants lightly but frequently. Too much nitrogen can burn plant roots and encourage the development of lots of leaves and only a few flowers or fruits.

Tipburn

SYMPTOMS AND CAUSE Plant leaves show yellowing or browning around their edges, and the tips of the leaves may shrivel and curl downward. Commonly called tipburn, this problem usually develops when plants are growing rapidly.

PLANTS AFFECTED Numerous plants develop symptoms of tipburn a couple of weeks after they are set in containers. The problem often can be traced to roots that were injured during trans-

planting, or containers that dry up daily, along with the roots right inside the pots. Spotty watering that does not thoroughly moisten the potting soil and roots also can lead to tipburned leaves.

WHAT TO DO Take measures to ensure that all of the plant's roots are given constant access to moisture and fertilizer. This may mean more attentive care for a short time, or you may need to shift the plants to larger pots. However, it is always a good idea to give the plants time to overcome the problem before repotting them. Light pruning of stems to reduce demands made on the roots also can be beneficial.

APPENDIX
SOURCES FOR PLANTS, SEEDS AND SUPPLIES

Vegetable and Flower Seeds

W. Atlee Burpee Co.
300 Park Ave.
Warminster, PA 18974
800-888-1447

Cook's Garden
P.O. Box 535
Londonderry, VT 05148
802-824-3400

Johnny's Selected Seeds
Foss Hill Rd.
Albion, ME 04910
207-437-4301

Nichols Garden Nursery
1190 North Pacific Hwy.
Albany, OR 97321
541-928-9280

Park Seed
1 Parkton Ave.
Greenwood, SC 29647
800-845-3369

Pinetree Garden Seeds
P.O. Box 300
New Gloucester, ME
04260
207-926-3400

Shepherd's Garden Seeds
30 Irene St.
Torrington, CT 06790
860-482-3638

Perennials and Shrubs

Bluestone Perennials
7213 Middle Ridge Rd.
Madison, OH 44057
800-852-5243

Busse Gardens
5873 Oliver Ave. SW
Cokato, MN 55321
800-544-3192

Carroll Gardens
444 E. Main St.
Westminster, MD 21157
800-638-6334

Joy Creek Nursery
20300 NW Watson Rd.
Scappoose, OR 97056
503-543-7474

Klehm Nursery
4210 N. Duncan Rd.
Champaign, IL 61821
800-553-3715

Logee's Greenhouses
141 North St.
Danielson, CT 06239
203-774-8038

Milaeger's Gardens
4838 Douglas Ave.
Racine, WI 53402
800-669-9956

Niche Gardens
111 Dawson Rd.
Chapel Hill, NC 27516
919-967-0078

Siskiyou Rare Plant
Nursery
2825 Cummings Rd.
Medford, OR 97501
503-772-6846

Andre Viette Nursery
Rt. 1, Box 16
Fishersville, VA 22939
703-942-2118

Wayside Gardens
1 Garden Ln.
Hodges, SC 26965
800-845-1124

White Flower Farm
P.O. Box 50
Litchfield, CT 06759
800-503-9624

Woodlanders
1128 Colleton Ave
Aiken, SC 28901
803-648-7522

Bulbs

The Daffodil Mart
85 Broad St.
Torrington, CT
06790-6668
800-255-2852

Dutch Gardens
P.O. Box 200
Adelphia, NJ 07710
800-818-3861

McClure & Zimmerman
P.O. Box 368
Friesland, WI 53935
414-326-4220

Van Bourgondien
P.O. Box 1000
Babylon, NY 11702
800-622-9997

Roses

Antique Rose Emporium
Rt. 5, Box 143
Brenham, TX 77833
409-836-9051

Jackson & Perkins
P.O. Box 1028
Medford, OR 97501
800-292-4769

Royall River Roses
70 New Gloucester Rd.
North Yarmouth, ME
04097
800-820-5830

Roses of Yesterday
& Today
803 Brown's Valley Rd.
Watsonville, CA 95076
408-724-2755

Herb Plants

Mountain Valley Growers
38325 Pepperweed Rd.
Squaw Valley, CA 93675
209-338-2775

Sandy Mush Herb
Nursery
316 Surrett Cove Rd.
Leicester, NC 28748
704-683-2014

Sunnybrook Farms
9448 Mayfield Rd.
P.O. Box 6
Chesterland, OH 44026
216-729-7232

Fruits

Northwoods Nursery
27635 S. Oglesby Rd.
Canby, OR 97013
503-266-5432

Raintree Nursery
391 Butts Rd.
Morton, WA 98356
360-496-6400

Stark Brothers
P.O. Box 10
Louisiana, MO 63353
800-325-4150

Bananas

Brudy's Exotics
P.O. Box 820874
Houston, TX 77282-0874
800 926 7333
Web Site Catalog:
http://www.brudys-
exotics.com

Stokes Tropicals
P.O. Box 9868
New Iberia, LA 70562-
9868
800 624-9706
Web Site Catalog:
http://www.stokes-
tropicals.com

Fertilizers

Gardener's Supply Co.
128 Intervale Rd.
Burlington, VT 05041
800-234-6630

Gardens Alive!
5100 Schenley Place
Lawrenceburg, IN 47025
812-537-8650

Peaceful Valley Farm
Supply
P.O. Box 2209
Grass Valley, CA 95945
916-272-4769

Irrigation Equipment

Gardener's Supply Co.
128 Intervale Road
Burlington, VT 05041
800-234-6630

Worm's Way
3151 S. Highway 446
Bloomington, IN 47401
800-274-9676

Water Gardening Plants and Equipment

Lilypons Water Gardens
P.O. Box 10
Buckeystown, MD 21717
*(also locations in Texas
and California)*
800-723-7667

Perry's Water Gardens
1831 Leatherman Gap Rd.
Franklin, NC 28734
704-369-2056

CONTAINER GARDEN PLANT LISTS

Perennials		
common name	**Latin name**	**best cultivars**
Achillea	*Achillea millefolium*	
Agapanthus	*Agapanthus* species	'Bressingham Blue' 'Headbourne Hybrids'
Alyssum	*Aurinia saxatilis*	
Artemisia	*Artemisia* species	'Silver Queen' and 'Silver King'
Bergenia	*Bergenia* species	
Bougainvillea	*Bougainvillea* hybrids	
Candytuft	*Iberis sempervirens*	
Carnation	*Dianthus caryophyllus*	'Chabaud', 'Burpee's Super Giants'
Chrysanthemum	*Dendranthema* hybrids	
Clivia	*Clivia miniata*	
Clematis	*Clematis* species	
Coral bells	*Heuchera* species	
Coreopsis	*Coreopsis* species	'Domino'
Daylily	*Hemerocallis* hybrids	'Stella D'Oro', 'Pardon Me', 'Happy Returns'
English ivy	*Hedera helix*	
Fern	numerous species	
Flax, New Zealand	*Phormium tenax*	
Foxglove	*Digitalis grandiflora*	
Fuchsia	*Fuchsia* hybrids	
Geranium	*Pelargonium* species	'Golden Crest'
Helianthemum	*Helianthemum nummularium*	
Hosta	*Hosta* species	
Lamb's-ear	*Stachys byzantina*	
Lamium	*Lamium maculatum*	
Liriope	*Liriope* species	
Lychnis	*Lychnis coronaria*	
Penstemon	*Penstemon digitalis*	'Husker Red'
Phlox, creeping	*Phlox subulata*	
Primula	*Primula* species	'Barnhaven'
Rudbeckia	*Rudbeckia* species	'Goldsturm'
Salvia	*Salvia* species	'May Night'
Saxifrage	*Saxifrage* species	
Sedum	*Sedum* species	
Verbena	*Verbena* species	'Homestead Purple'
Vinca minor, vinca major	*Vinca* species	
Viola	*Viola tricolor*	

Annual Flowers

common name	Latin name
Ageratum	*Ageratum houstonianum*
Alyssum, sweet	*Lobularia maritima*
Aster China	*Aster* species
Baby's breath	*Gypsophilia elegans*
Begonia	*Begonia semperflorens*
Bidens	*Bidens ferulifolia*
Black-eyed Susan vine	*Thunbergia alata*
Brachycome	*Brachycome iberidifolia*
Browallia	*Browallia speciosa*
Calendula	*Calendula officinalis*
Candytuft	*Iberis umbellata*
Celosia	*Celosia argentea plumosa*
Coleus	*Solenostemon scutellarioides*
Cosmos	*Cosmos* species
Dianthus	*Dianthus* hybrids
Dusty Miller	*Senecio cineraria*
Forget-me-not	*Myosotis* species
Gomphrena	*Gomphrena* species
Heliotrope	*Heliotropium arborescens*
Impatiens	*Impatiens* hybrids
Lantana	*Lantana camara*
Lobelia	*Lobelia erinus*
Marigold	*Tagetes* species
Melampodium	*Melampodium paludosum*
Morning glory	*Ipomoea* species
Nasturtium	*Tropaeolum* species
Nemesia	*Nemesia* hybrids
Nicotiana	*Nicotiana* hybrids
Nierembergia	*Nierembergia hippomanica*
Nolana	*Nolana* species
Pansy	*Viola x wittrockiana*
Pentas	*Pentas lanceolata*
Petunia	*Petunia* hybrids
Phlox	*Phlox drummondii*
Polka dot plant	*Hypoestes phyllostachya*
Portulaca	*Portulaca grandiflora*
Salvia	*Salvia* species
Sanvitalia	*Sanvitalia procumbens*
Scaevola	*Scaevola* species
Scarlet runner bean	*Phaseolus* species
Schizanthus	*Schizanthus pinnatus*
Snapdragon	*Antirrhinum majus*
Stock	*Matthiola Incana*
Sunflower	*Helianthus annuus*
Sweet pea	*Lathyrus odoratus*
Torenia	*Torenia* species
Verbena	*Verbena* hybrids
Vinca	*Catharanthus roseus*
Zinnia	*Zinnia* species

Bulbs, Corms and Tubers

Aconite, winter	*Eranthis hyemalis*
Allium	*Allium* species
Amaryllis	*Hippeastrum* hybrids
Anemone	*Anemone coronaria*
Basket flower	*Hymenocallis narcissiflora*
Begonia, tuberous	*Begonia* hybrids
Caladium	*Caladium* species
Crocus	*Crocus* species
Daffodil and narcissus	*Narcissus* species
Dahlia	*Dahlia* hybrids
Fritillary	*Fritillaria* species
Glory-of-the-snow	*Chinodoxa* species
Grape hyacinth	*Muscari* species
Hyacinth	*Hyacinthus orientalis*
Iris	*Iris* species
Lily	*Lilium* hybrids
Peacock orchid	*Acidanthera bicolor* aka *Gladiolus callianthus*
Puschinkia	*Puschkinia* species
Scilla	*Scilla* species
Snowdrops	*Galanthus* species
Sweet Potato	*Ipomoea batatas*
Tulip	*Tulipa* hybrids

Vegetables

Bean, snap	*Phaseolus vulgaris*
Beet	*Beta vulgaris*
Broccoli	*Brassica oleracea Italica*
Bunching onion	*Allium fistulosum*
Cabbage	*Brassica oleracea Capitata*
Carrot	*Daucus carota sativa*
Cauliflower	*Brassica oleracea Botrytis*
Celery	*Apium graveolens*
Chard, Swiss	*Beta vulgaris cicla*
Chinese cabbage	*Brassica rapa Pekinensis*
Cucumber	*Cucumis sativus*
Eggplant	*Solanum melongena*
Lettuce	*Lactuca sativa*
Mesclun	Mix of: *Latuca sativa, Chichorium endivia, Brassica rapa, Lepidium sativum, Eruca vesicaria sativa, Valerianella locusta, Anthriscus cerefolium*
Okra	*Abelmoschus esculentus*
Pea	*Piscum sativum*
Pepper	*Capsicum annuum*
Radish	*Raphanus sativus*
Spinach	*Spinacia oleracea*
Squash	*Cucurbita pepo, Cucurbita maxima, Cucurbita moschata*
Tomato	*Lycopersicon esculentum*

Roses, Shrubs and Trees	
Roses, hybrid tea	'Miss All-American Beauty' (pink) 'Double Delight' (pink blend) 'Olympiad' (red) 'Tropicana' (coral)
Roses, floribunda	'Iceberg' (white) 'Europeana' (red) 'Sexy Rexy' (pink)
Roses, miniature	'Red Cascade' (red) 'Giggles' (pink) 'Rise 'n' Shine' (yellow) 'Pacesetter' (white)
Roses, species	*Rosa chinensis* 'Mutabilis' *Rosa moyesii* 'Geranium'
Aucuba	*Aucuba japonica* 'Variegata'
Azalea	*Rhododendron* hybrids
Bamboo	*Arundinaria* and *Bambusa* species
Boxwood	*Buxus* species
Dogwood	*Cornus florida*
Dwarf Alberta Spruce	*Picea glauca* 'Conica'
Flowering Maple	*Abutilon hybridum*
Heather	*Calluna vulgaris*
Heath	*Erica carnea*
Hibiscus	*Hibiscus rosa-sinensis*
Holly	*Ilex* species
Hydrangea	*Hydrangea* species
Japanese Maple	*Acer palmatum*
Juniper	*Juniperus* species
Mugo Pine	*Pinus mugo* var. *mugo*
Pomegranate	*Punica granatum*
Wisteria	*Wisteria* species

Herbs	
Basil	*Ocimum basilicum*
Bay	*Laurus noblis*
Chervil	*Anthriscus cerefolium*
Chives	*Allium schoenoprasum*
Cilantro (Coriander)	*Coriandrum sativum*
Dill	*Anethum graveolens*
French tarragon	*Artemesia dracunculus*
Garlic	*Allium sativum*
Garlic Chives	*Allium tuberosum*
Lavender	*Lavendula angustifolia*
Lemongrass	*Cymbopogon citratus*
Lemon verbena	*Aloysia triphylla*
Mexican marigold	*Tagetes lucida*
Mints	*Mentha* species
Majoram	*Origanum onites*
Oregano	*Origanum vulgare*
Parsley	*Petroselinum crispum*
Rosemary	*Rosmarinus officinalis*
Sage	*Salvia officinalis*
Thymes	*Thymus* species

Fruit	
Apple	*Malus pumila*
Banana	*Musa acuminata*
Blueberry	*Vaccinium corymbosum,* *Vaccinium ashei*
Citrus	*Citrus* species
Cherry	*Prunus avium, Prunus cerasus*
Fig	*Ficus carica*
Kumquat	*Fortunella crassifolia*
Melon	*Cucumis melo, Citrullus vulgaris*
Peach	*Prunus persica*
Pomegranate	*Punica granatum*
Strawberry	*Fragaria* species

U.S. Plant Hardiness
Zone Map

Zone 1: Below –50° F
Zone 2: –50° to –40°
Zone 3: –40° to –30°
Zone 4: –30° to –20°
Zone 5: –20° to –10°
Zone 6: –10° to 0°
Zone 7: 0° to 10°
Zone 8: 10° to 20°
Zone 9: 20° to 30°
Zone 10: 30° to 40°
Zone 11: Above 40

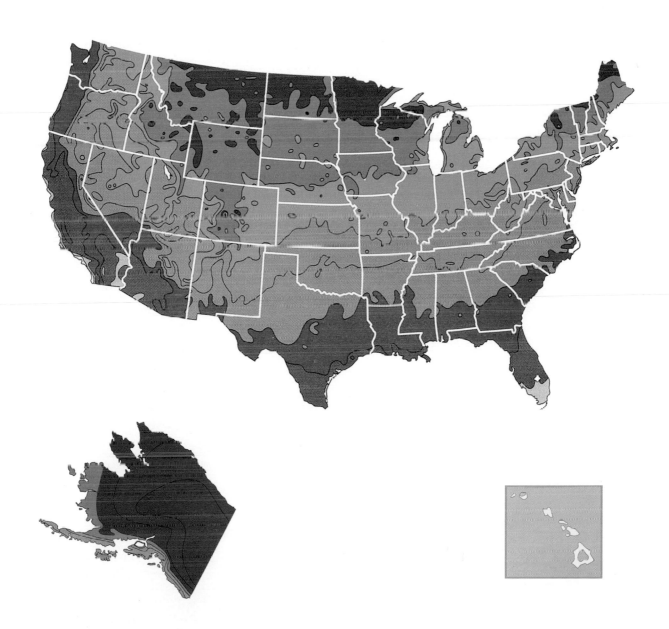

INDEX